Ranunculus – *a popular pond plant.*

THE INTERPET
Bumper
GUIDE TO
GARDEN
PONDS

Huge slabs of rock create a dramatic cascade.

INTERPET

Compiled by
Dick Mills

Japanese-style ponds are popular with Koi-keepers.

THE INTERPET
Bumper
GUIDE TO
GARDEN
PONDS

INTERPET

An **INTERPET** ▶▷ Book

ISBN 1-902389-79-4

All correspondence concerning the content of this volume
should be addressed to Interpet Ltd.

Credits

Editor: Anne McDowall
Designers: Louise Bruce and Tim Scott
Colour reproductions: Tempus Litho, Melbourne Graphics Ltd.,
Scantrans Pte Ltd.
Filmset: SX Composing Ltd.
Printed in China

Authors

Dick Mills, who has compiled this book, and written many of the chapters, has been keeping fishes for over 30 years, during which time he has written many articles for aquatic hobby magazines as well as 12 books. He has been a Council member of the Federation of British Aquatic Societies for 20 years.

David Papworth, who has written many of the chapters on pond design and construction and Part Three on plants for the pond, is the author of a number of books on horticultural subjects and regularly contributes articles and illustrations to gardening and DIY books and magazines.

Barry James, who has written the chapters on water gardens and filters and aeration and much of Part Four on pond fish, runs his own aquatic nurseries as well as regularly contributing features and photographs to the aquatic press and acting as a consultant worldwide on aquatic matters.

Dr Chris Andrews, who has written some of the chapters on pond fish, is well known for his magazine articles and appearances on television in connection with the fishkeeping hobby. Previously responsible for the Aquarium at London Zoo, he is now at the National Aquarium, Baltimore, USA.

Take a seat and admire this well-stocked pond.

Contents

INTRODUCTION

A garden pond has many different attractions for different people. Apart from its visual appeal, the garden pond becomes a constantly changing, living focal point in even the smallest garden and there is no denying the soothing effect of the sound of trickling water from fountain or waterfall.

However, the pond is also a highly complex unit that demands close attention to many separate components. You will need basic physics, biology, mathematics and a growing awareness of water chemistry, together with an aesthetic eye for artistic arrangements, and maybe an inventive mind, to create the necessary excuses for spending more time than you ever thought possible around the pond's banks!

In order for the pond to look, and perform, its best throughout the year, try to acquire as much knowledge as possible about all the different aspects of such an exciting feature. In return for your labours, you will derive great pleasure from admiring the beauty of aquatic plants, the colours of the fishes and the variety of wildlife that a pond attracts.

Obviously, an appreciation of garden plants, and how to incorporate them around the pond, will play an important part, and so, too, will any existing knowledge of fishkeeping; a pond will get the indoor fishkeeper out of doors a lot more often! Of course, experience of either of these two topics is not essential, but when you decide to build a pond, study the basics long before lifting a single turf or buying your first fishing gnome!

This book will show you the different types of pond (and their inhabitants) available, and how to design, build and maintain them. Hopefully, it will help you to succeed in the water garden of your choice, but what it cannot do is to cure you of the grip which water gardening will have on you once you get started.

Right: *A pond adds a fresh dimension to a garden, particularly if it also includes a waterfall.*

PART 1

POND AND WATER GARDEN DESIGN

The addition of a water feature to any garden will change its appearance dramatically and, with the help of this book, for the better. Styles of pond can vary enormously, from the sublime to the ridiculous, or, to put it another way, from the suitable to the downright unsuitable.

There is little point in 'over-designing' the pond for a small town garden; nor does every design suit every situation, as each has to be judged on what other garden features are already in existence, or planned for the future. Formal designs may be more simple to install, but may be at odds with a more informal existing garden layout. To take another example, although biggest is best (as far as maintenance and stable water conditions are concerned), a 'wall-to-wall' pond will tend to dominate, leaving little room for other garden features.

There are also more practical considerations: cost is usually the first of these, but cheap materials are not usually the best. Inexpensive plastic pond liners are often short-lived, with any exposed parts particularly prone to ultra-violet damage from the sun's rays or spoiling by frost.

You may think that solid concrete is the answer, as far as permanence is concerned; this may often be so, but two points should be borne in mind. Although well suited for straight-edged, formal designs, concrete is much more difficult to use where more curving, informal designs are needed; the question of soil condition is important too, for wherever there is a risk of subsidence concrete will crack with disastrous results.

The first question to ask yourself is what type of pond you want. Is it to be a 'nature pond', an integrated fish and plants pond or one intended primarily to accommodate fish? It pays to make such decisions well in advance – it could prevent a lot of problems and expense in the future.

Right: *Careful planning is essential to create a good-looking and fully integrated water garden.*

Natural ponds

The term 'natural pond' implies an artificially constructed pond that follows the same natural pattern of development, and provides the same habitat for wildlife, plants, insects and seasonal visitors, as might a pond occurring in nature. But just how does a natural pond differ from any other?

Ponds designed for fish culture conform to certain parameters – water depth, water surface-area etc – in order for the fish to survive all year round. A natural pond can be of any size, as it may not be so critical to indigenous life-forms if it does partially dry up in high summer, or freeze nearly solid in deepest winter. The cross-sectional profile should be shallow rather than steep-sided (although some deeper areas of water can be included for better stability of water conditions) to allow easy access for amphibious animals, insects and birds. If you decide to turn an existing steep-sided pond into a nature pond then some sloping ramps (semi-immersed logs, for example) should be installed to provide such facilities. A 'beach area' (another very practical means of access) is easily constructed using a layer of large pebbles extending well into the shallow water.

The surrounds of a natural pond can be left uncultivated (but not unmanaged) to a certain extent, and here a bog or marshy area can be of enormous benefit to wildlife (although possibly inconvenient to any approaching humans). The easiest way to cater for true marshy or bog plants, is to extend the pond liner well beyond the pond perimeter into a lower surrounding 'moat' and re-cover with coarse matting and a deep layer of soil. Keep this area very wet (there is no need for any water to be visible above ground) and plant with suitable species (see pages 118-121).

The area surrounding the pond should provide as much cover as possible to protect amphibious animals from predators as they emerge from or approach the pond. The last thing a natural pond needs is the obvious mark of Man, so no fancy edging paving slabs; natural turf is best if you must have the edges clearly defined.

Aquatic plants in the pond can be grown in containers (if water depth is sufficient) or in soil placed in pockets incorporated into the liner – the shallow design of the pond will prevent too much spillage of soil into the main body of the pond. Containerized plants are preferable – faster-growing plants (likely to become rampant at the slightest opportunity) are much more manageable when grown in pots, and cleaning out the pond is easier, too, with less risk of puncturing the liner while doing so.

Positioning the pond may not be as critical as for a fish-holding pond but, while nearby trees may give partial shade, their roots may pierce a plastic liner, or crack a concrete pond. You will need to think carefully about siting the pond, so that it suits not only the demands of wildlife for seclusion, but also your own interests in terms of visibility and access.

Stocking the natural pond can be difficult, especially in smaller ponds where there is simply no room for every kind of inhabitant to find its own niche. Large fish will eat smaller ones (who have no easy escape areas) but, on the other hand, a population of small fish will soon denude the pond of its insect and small amphibious life. One answer would be to have two ponds, (ambitious plans often begin like this!) interconnected by a cascade or stream, with fish in one pond only. Birds will most certainly visit the pond to drink and bathe, but, unless the pond is large with easy flying access (no nearby trees), it is unlikely that wildfowl will be among your guests. Other aquatic life-forms, such as frogs, toads and newts are dealt with in Appendix One on pages 218-221.

Right: *The plants and gently sloping lawn surrounding this pond provide well-protected, and easy-access, points for wildlife.*

Water garden ponds

This type of pond is probably the ideal to which every water-gardener aspires (at least at the outset). Who can deny its appeal, with fishes and pond plants complementing each other, marginal plants making the transition from land to water not only gradually but colourfully too? With fountains playing, waterfalls and cascades adding genuine 'water music' and maybe a patio area within easy sight of the pond, the picture is truly complete. But, as you will see, this happy scene cannot come about without a great deal of work.

It is easy to assume that a pond is merely a slice of aquatic life captured in the convenience of the garden; unfortunately, unlike the natural pond, it cannot always be left to Mother Nature if it is to be attractive throughout all the seasons of the year. This is particularly true in respect of keeping water conditions stable and in good condition.

True wildlife aquatic settings are, to some extent, self-preserving – wind, rain and natural waterflows help to clean the water, and the fish can usually swim away to find a better environment, or food supply, should they need to do so. In the static waters of a pond the maintenance of good water conditions, and prudent stocking of compatible species, are only two of the many responsibilities of the pondkeeper.

It is important to realize that *everything* that goes into the pond will affect the water conditions to some extent, for better or worse. This includes not only fish and plants, but also leaves and berries from nearby trees, or insecticides blown over from a neighbour's garden. Additionally, fish kept in captivity also cause their own environment to deteriorate, as they produce waste, often toxic-forming materials, through the very process of living. This means that the pond will require additional help in maintaining itself – pumps and filters and so on – and will need to be within easy reach of

electricity and, if possible, a ready supply of water.

Choose the site carefully to ensure that the pond has more than a fair chance of survival, and of supporting itself. How it looks within the garden may well be uppermost in the fishkeeper's mind, but this may not always fit in with what is best for the pond. There is little point in siting a pond beautifully if it soon degenerates into a decaying, foul muddy mess through lack of understanding of its basic needs.

Trees, particularly large ones, can be a pond's worst enemy, although apparently providing an

ideal backdrop. They pose several threats to the pond's continuing well-being. As mentioned previously, everything that enters the pond will affect it in some way; sadly, very little tree-based material is beneficial except, perhaps, for the small insects and caterpillars that fall from its branches. Any autumn leaves, berries and flowers falling into the pond, if not poisonous in themselves, will decompose, using up valuable oxygen in the process. Tree roots can easily puncture a pond liner or crack concrete walls; this can be guarded against to some extent by adding some

Above: This pond receives its necessary share of direct sunshine by virtue of its open position, but is well sheltered from winds.

padding – typically to the excavated hole before positioning the liner. Planted ponds need a good deal of sunshine if a pleasing show of water-lilies is required; another argument for a reasonably open position and against siting a pond near trees. The only good thing a tree can offer is shelter from strong wind but a nearby hedge, fence or shrubbery would provide just as good a defence, and pose a barrier to herons.

Koi ponds

It may seem a trifle pedantic to separate the Koi pond from any other fish-holding pond, but these superb fishes require slightly different conditions, which may not be available in existing ponds. Koi-keeping is more of a specialist interest than other forms of general fishkeeping, although serious Goldfish keepers might not agree!

Koi are large fish and require both space and depth if they are to realize their full potential; it is not uncommon for Koi to reach 60 cm (24in) or more in length, so living quarters need to be spacious in order to keep a reasonable number of fish. Added to this, Koi have extremely healthy appetites which, again, can cause problems: they produce quantities of waste materials that necessitate a very efficient filtration system; their omnivorous diet includes vegetable matter, which can make choosing pond plants difficult.

In order to accommodate Koi in a healthy environment, the pond has to be large and, just as important, have a minimum depth of around 1.5m (5ft) to allow safe over-wintering. The filtration system (itself at least one-third pond size) is best planned and installed from the outset, rather than added on to an existing pond. There is no need for a large filtration plant alongside the pond to look unsightly; often it can be covered by decking to form a very comfortable seating area – an excellent vantage point from which to admire the fish on long, lazy summer evenings.

Koi-keeping may seem problematic and technical, but these attractive fish bring an extra dimension to the pond, especially to the totally committed – the culture of the Orient. Koi originate in Japan, where they have been bred for many years. They are best viewed from above (their colour patterns are chosen for clarity and design with this in mind) and water clarity is essential, so that the fish can be seen clearly at all times. Such is the attraction of Koi, and all things pertaining to them, that many Koi-owners design the pond and its surroundings to reflect the fishes' original home, with carefully chosen plants, oriental features (such as stone lanterns, water basins and 'deer-scarers') and, if space allows, bridges and pagodas. However, not every Koi pond needs to be surrounded by

Right: *Pagoda and conifers reflect the Japanese theme to this Koi pond. (Note the cleverly hidden pond filter on the far right.)*

oriental artifacts and many blend in quite happily in any garden.

Like all bodies of water, a Koi pond can be a source of danger, especially to children; low shrubs around the perimeter will act both as a warning of the pond's existence and as a natural defensive barrier. Alternatively, a raised pond is entirely feasible, and may be safer.

Because of their size, Koi ponds are often built either in concrete, double brick or block construction, although in areas where subsidence is commonplace, specially tailored liners are more practical. Drainage and filtration systems are best integrated into the pond during construction, and the steep-sided walls allow the fishkeeper to get even closer to the fish, which soon become hand-tame. Despite their size, Koi are at risk from wading herons (their greatest predator), but one or two sides of the pond can incorporate some vertical physical barriers.

Small formal ponds

If a small garden of some 12m (40ft) square is to contain a pond and a formal arrangement, it needs careful planning. The formal shape requires a pattern that can be either symmetrical or not, but usually incorporating straight lines and regular curves in the layout. It can be classical in concept, like part of a Grecian temple, or just an arrangement of definite squares, rectangles, circles or half-circles of paving, planting or areas of water, put together to provide a complete scene to suit your taste.

With such a small area and usually with restricted access it is wise to forgo a lawn and use paving instead. With the variety of different types and colours available now, there is no need for an area of paving to look boring; it can be divided up into sections of contrasting colour or shape to give variety.

The pond can be simple or dramatic, sunk below ground level or raised up, with fountains or waterfalls to provide movement of water that is in scale with the size of the garden, and room for a few choice aquatic plants and a small selection of fancy fishes. Constructions around the pond must harmonize with the garden style: simple paving-slab bridges and stepping stones fit into a formal scheme far better than their rustic counterparts, and planting in the garden needs to be fairly ordered and regular in shape and type. Conifers in pots will not drop their leaves in autumn, yet will give height and foliage colour all the year round. Bright colours can be provided by using bulbs for spring blooms and annuals for summer and autumn brilliance, leaving the evergreens to carry their foliage through the winter until spring returns again.

Where there is a change in the level of the site it should be emphasized with steps and walls constructed in a material that links with other garden constructions and with the bricks or stone of the house, in order to keep the formal look to the garden.

Left: *An angular, L-shaped pool with straight edges and regular paving makes a very formal area only softened by the plants and the movement and splash of the water. On the opposite page the hard lines have been muted by the foliage.*

Right: *Use a bare wall to make a water feature by building up two semicircular pools and a wall-mounted fountain. Evergreens are used to provide an all-year-round background without the autumn problem of leaves, and placed to give a near symmetrical design.*

Small informal ponds

Ponds of informal design need to look very natural, as if they have just been picked up from the wild and dropped into the garden. This can be quite difficult to achieve in a garden that is only some 12m (40ft) square. One important factor is to ensure that the pond does not overpower the rest of the garden by its size, nor should it be too small and tucked away in a corner. The surface reserved for sitting and walking on should look natural and casual, with the use of as much natural material as possible. If it is necessary to use regular precast paving, then use it in a random fashion to avoid any feeling of formality. Gravel, sections cut from tree trunks and random pieces of stone can be used, separately or mixed, to give an informal air to the garden and the pond surround.

The pond can have a curved irregular shape, but keep it simple to avoid pockets of water becoming stagnant. Waterfalls also need to look as natural as possible. Constructions in the pond can be quite rustic in feeling; use wood to make bridges, and large lumps of rock or boulders to form edges and provide cascades for the water to tumble down.

Another way to keep a natural look and avoid the tailored effect of mown grass is to make an irregular shape close to the water that is close cut, but leave a surrounding section to grow higher; this will soften the appearance and help to keep a pleasant informal arrangement. Planting also needs to be kept looking informal, with tufts of plants and casual clumps of shrubs and trees. Try to keep to evergreens to avoid the leaf problem in autumn. Flowers look happiest if they are dotted casually around the garden in a disordered way, like a meadow of wild flowers.

Slopes or irregularities in the soil levels can be used to advantage to make mounds and small outcrops of stone, to emphasize the natural feel of the garden. The spoil from the pond excavation can be used to good effect by building up a small hillock, and this gives some height to what may be an otherwise flat garden site. Do not let water drain from such a new rise into the pond, though.

Above: *An informal look is achieved by keeping the curves natural and the planting simple and well positioned without overcrowding.*

Left: *In a simple design the spoil from the pool is used to make a mound covered with rocks for a waterfall; the lack of straight edges helps to give a casual look.*

Far left: *An ambitious design with a bridge to the raised section, sheltered with evergreen planting and keeping a suitably natural feel with the irregular arrangement of the paving.*

Small semi-formal ponds

Right: *A sloping site is used to make a stepped arrangement, allowing water and two styles of paving to break up a hard area; planting may be restricted to forming a background.*

Far right: *With hexagonal paving an irregular edge is given to the pool; stepping stones and a fountain also make the design less rigid. The bare wall has been covered with a creeper.*

The semi-formal garden often has the best of both the formal and the informal world. When used well the mixture of natural arrangement and ordered constructions can be most effective. It is less hard-looking than the formal garden and yet is not wild enough to be classed as informal, having the appearance of a piece of man-made construction surrounded by nature; this echoes the house structure surrounded by or neighboured by nature in the garden.

Paving may be regular or irregular in shape, man-made or natural. Walls can be brick, stone or timber, and the planting may take the form of either natural disorder or a more restricting order. But whatever style is followed it is important to strike a balance. To design this semi-formal type of garden in a small 12m (40ft) square takes some skill, but keep the pond shape simple, with either a fountain or a waterfall (of formal or informal concept, whether a natural cascade or a concrete structure) to give movement to the water.

Pond constructions can use a variety of materials: wood, stone, concrete or brick. It is wise to relate some of the materials to the house so that there is some connection between the two, whether it is bricks or stone that make the transition.

Plants can be neatly confined to containers, left to ramble along a boundary, or even grouped into irregular clumps. Planting in the water should allow the leaf and flower shapes to be seen clearly as well as the fishes in the water, which can be either fancy or not, according to the owner's tastes. Choose evergreens where possible, to avoid leaves falling into the pond during autumn. Provide colour by growing annuals, perennials, bulbs, shrubs and flowering trees, to give some interest throughout the year. In a garden of this size, the inclusion of a number of heavily scented flowers can give particular delight during the spring and summer months.

Left: *The mixture of formal and informal styles can be most attractive, keeping the advantages of simple shapes with a natural look.*

Medium-sized formal ponds

A medium-sized garden can incorporate a larger pond and a more complex system of moving water involving streams and waterfalls. This type of design can happily form part of a larger garden, and here the design is concentrated in a squarish section that contains the water garden some 18m (60ft) square.

The use of regular geometric shapes helps to give formality to the design, whether it is a series of interlocking squares and rectangles, circles or a simple symmetrical shape. The water element can be raised above the ground to form a dramatic tower system gushing water; a low container that allows one to sit upon the edge; or even a below-ground-level construction that is meant to be viewed from above.

The use of different materials will help to provide visual interest. Railway sleepers set into gravel, paving mixed with brick, concrete with stone chips, or reconstituted stone with natural stone, can all give variety of texture and colour to set off the sparkle of water. Pond construction can be made of the same materials or contrasting with a random pile of natural rocks. Water can be moved through fountains or over waterfalls using different forms to give a dramatic or interesting effect to the overall design.

Low-growing plants can soften hard paving or gravel; tall trees give instant height if bought as container plants or as specimens several years old; tubs of plants can be moved from one place to another to give variety whenever the owner chooses; and climbers trained up trellis or large plain walls can screen out unwanted views and provide a measure of privacy. Annuals, perennials, bulbs and shrubs will give a brilliant display in spring, summer and autumn, leaving the evergreens to continue through the winter (with their different shapes and wide variety of hues of green, yellow, blue and red foliage).

The cost of such a pond can vary considerably, depending on the materials and the amount used, but by choosing wisely you can make an exciting pond setting without too much strain on the purse.

Below: *A formal double circular pool with the jungle air of a thatched summerhouse and bamboos.*

Above: *The careful use of old railway sleepers and brick paving makes this design unusual and interesting.*

Below: *A very formal arrangement sees the plants carefully matched and placed in a regular pattern.*

25

Medium-sized informal ponds

The opportunities offered by having a medium-sized area of about 18m (60ft) square in which to design an informal pond are many. The main aim is to look as if a slice or section of nature has been lifted out and placed in your garden. This entails great care in the placing of the various elements that will make up the area. The shapes, particularly that of the pond, need to be casual in appearance and as un-manmade as possible.

For a special effect, the human touch can give a dramatic gesture, like a marble statue set in a natural-looking grotto. Use natural materials, and avoid concrete and regular patterns, especially for seating areas; use timber, stone, gravel and grass. The timber needs to be discrete, not raw, freshly sawn timber that stands out like a sore thumb; treat new wood with a preservative that is dull in

colour, to make it blend into the overall design of the pond area.

Pond shapes should be curved, and the curves need to be gentle, as if worn with time. Keep any straight lines to constructions such as bridges, piers or landing stages. Large pieces of stone should be used in construction work as this helps give the garden a sense of scale. Large logs of timber will give the feeling of strength; and islands need to be big enough to sit on, or to grow a specimen tree for shade.

Planting should look casual and without order, some close together and others wide apart. Use the more natural plants to form clumps and groups, instead of exotic-looking specimens placed obviously at a focal point. The use of evergreens will cut down problems with the autumn leaf fall, and colour can be provided by

using bulbs, annuals, perennials, flowering shrubs and trees.

Use any slope or variation in the levels to advantage, to make a more dramatic effect with mounds, banks and hollows or (with the use of stone) to make an outcrop of rock or a scree area. The spoil from the pond excavation can be used to build up a hillock for a cascade.

Above: *Under the riot of colourful plants there is a careful design contriving to give a natural appearance to the water and stone.*

Below: *A free-form pool that has an island coupled to the garden by a wooden bridge screened with casual evergreen planting gives this garden a natural and pleasing appearance.*

Medium-sized semi-formal ponds

Above: *A fine mixture of formal and informal elements make this a very pleasant garden.*

Left: *A simple design involving a paved area round a regular shaped pool next to a beach, with a planting of evergreens to give a natural background.*

Right: *A stone figure in a small pool and flanked with mirrors can give the illusion of more space.*

To design a medium-sized garden with a water feature in a semi-formal manner will mean mixing elements that can look opposed in style. This can succeed if there is a balance: for example, a formal element can be treated as an extension of the existing formality of the house structure, and a terrace, deck area, patio or sitting space can use regular shapes and obviously man-made materials that echo those used in the house construction. This major element can then blend into or be placed next to an informal pond or planting space, where one can step from a rectangular area designed for entertaining onto gravel or pebbles laid in a random manner next to a curved stretch of water that contains a formal fountain and is surrounded by a mixture of wild and specimen planting. This mixture needs care and skill so that it does not look too confusing with everything vying for attention. The more dominant areas need playing down. With the right use of materials, such as timber and stone, the garden will look more relaxed and harmonious.

Pond shapes can be curved or straight, and edged with grass, paving or random boulders intermingled with pebbles, with water moving through fountains or waterfalls or a combination of both. Decks overlapping the pond can be used for barbecues, for sunbathing, or even as a site for a Jacuzzi. Constructions need to be in scale with the garden; avoid anything that is going to make the space look poky. It is better to have one large object – whether it is a rock, a statue, a water feature or a tree – rather than a collection of little ones.

Planting should be arranged to give interest in groups and variety in heights. There are plenty of trees with different forms that are evergreen, even a weeping cedar, which makes a fine feature by water, far superior to the popular weeping willow, which drops its leaves, and undermines the pond and any other building nearby with its roots. Use any natural slopes of the site or variations in level to make the garden and pool surround more sculptural and exciting.

Moving water features

Fountains and waterfalls do much to bring extra life and interest to the pond. They also provide a useful service in keeping the water aerated, a valuable asset on hot days when dissolved oxygen levels in the water are reduced. However, they are not entirely bound to the pond as a decorative and functional asset: many water gardens use water movement purely as a decorative feature, with many public fountains and pools being quite empty of fishes. In Spanish and Moorish gardens, the accent is more on soothing and cooling effects than on anything else; it should not be forgotten, either, that in much warmer climes, a fountain has practical functions too, as a source of drinking water or a place to wash.

In very small gardens the extension of the pond beyond its own perimeter may not be possible. In this case, a moving water feature may be limited to a simple fountain or, at most, a disguised water-return from an external filter. On an even smaller scale, a patio space may not be big enough to house a proper pond, but a millstone with water constantly flowing over it into a pebble-strewn basin will create the desired effect just the same.

Moving to the larger garden brings much more scope for creative ideas. Ponds can be interlinked with canals and waterways which can be used to mark boundaries between different areas of the garden. Designs can be entirely formal or emulate nature, but careful planning is always essential if the final result is not to look contrived. So much for general ideas, but not all ideas are workable straight from the initial paper plan.

Much depends, literally, on the 'lie of the land'. For natural-looking running water features, nothing can beat a diverted existing stream, but only a very small proportion of water-gardeners will have a natural source of running water at their disposal. Absolutely flat, or steeply sloping terrains also cause design problems, as they require soil to be added to (or shifted from) its original position. Gravity plays such a large part in water movement that it might seem logical to use it to its full advantage by having the pond at the lowest part of the garden, into which any watercourse finally empties. Unfortunately, gravity also affects everything else, and natural rainfall will tend to wash any loose soil, falling leaves and

Above: *Simple designs are often the best. A small fountain falling over a collection of pebbles makes a soothing patio water feature.*

Right: *Split-level pond designs are ideal for sloping sites and are often more interesting, and more natural, than a single, high waterfall.*

other small debris into the pond as well. It is better to reserve the lowest (and perhaps wettest) part of the garden for bog plants.

Waterfalls, with water falling clear of any obstruction, look impressive, but only in the right surroundings; an artificially constructed 'hill' on an otherwise flat landscape, just for the purpose of having a waterfall, will look more than a little unnatural. Better to have a less dramatic 'fall' of water, such as a series of small pools gently overflowing into each other until the main pond is reached. Another point to bear in mind is that although water movement is soothing during summer days, a large waterfall can generate a lot of noise at night.

Fountains
Operation of a fountain, cascade or waterfall is simplicity itself; a submerged pump recycles the pond's water up through a jet into the air, to the top of a watercourse or a higher pool, from where it falls or flows back into the pond again. The range of fountains is broad – from simple jets to whole rotating, multi-jet displays – and some designs even incorporate underwater, colour-changing light systems to bring further attraction

Above: *Siting the fountain so that its spray pattern is seen against a dark background greatly enhances its visual impact.*

Below: *Although of modest size, this water feature makes a quiet corner an ideal place to unwind from the day's worries.*

to your pond. Although many fountain-kit pumps have arrangements to allow separate water-feeds to filters, cascades etc., in water-moving features covering some distance it may be necessary to use separate pumps for cascades and waterfalls, as these require large amounts of water to give the right effect.

When selecting a fountain, be careful to choose the correct size for your pond. For example, the spray pattern from an overpowered pump may not be exactly the same as illustrated on the pump box when the water-flow is turned down to suit your size of pond. Apart from the height of the display (almost a status symbol with some pond-owners), the volume of water moved is also critical to the visual effect; fine jets produce height, but the droplets formed are often not noticeable from a distance.

Cascades

The decision to install a cascade often stems from the need to disguise the returning, cleaned water from an external filter system, often located at the top of a poolside rockery. Rather than have a plain pipe projecting over

the pond, why not direct the water back down a much more natural-looking cascade? Later, once your interest in water gardening really begins to expand, you can connect a second pond (on a slightly higher level) to the original by means of a watercourse. The simplest cascades are ready-made units of plastic, glass-fibre or re-constituted stone, but, although convenient and very quick to install, they are not altogether suitable for the larger water garden, where their small size becomes more and more visibly 'out of scale'. They can also be difficult to disguise when incorporating them into a 'natural' design. Where such a setting is needed, and space permits, then a liner water-course is the ideal answer – it gives greater creative freedom and is usually cheaper than using ready-made units.

Right: *Apart from a considerable amount of stonework, a powerful pump is also necessary to provide adequate water flow for this fall.*

Below: *This watercourse cuts a natural path in the landscape with a series of cascades that match the slope of the surrounding land.*

Waterfalls

Waterfalls can be great disappointments, usually (as in the case of fountains) because of undersized pumps or supply-hoses. It is surprising just how much *volume* (as opposed to pressure, in fountains) of water is needed to create even a fairly modest waterfall.

Just as with fountains, take precautions to avoid excessive water movement through the pond (especially one containing plants and fishes). To prevent plant-disturbing water currents occurring across the whole of the pond (and also to minimize friction-losses in the water supply pipework) the pump should be positioned as close to the bottom of the waterfall or cascade as possible. By

breaking the fall of a waterfall into a small pool first, you can avoid mud-churning disturbances occurring in the main pond. Fortunately, most fountains have their water intake directly beneath the 'fall-back' area, so, provided the fountain is placed in an area away from aquatic plants, particularly lilies, no harm should occur. If you are using a remote pump, avoid planting lilies between pump intake and fountain.

As you will see, the final visual effect of any moving water features, and their incorporation into the garden's overall design, depends on skill, artistic ability and careful planning (For practical advice on how to install fountains, cascades and waterfalls, see pages 50-55.)

Water gardens

In this section, we look at Oriental and Western water gardening, past and present, for ideas which can be adapted to make an effective and appropriate setting for a Koi pond.

Western gardens are admired for their formal beauty. While this means that their layouts are generally based on traditional geometrical designs, they do vary considerably: each garden is very much the creation of the individual gardener. A Japanese garden, however – although just as much a personal expression of its maker – is designed to reflect the natural landscape of Japan. It represents in miniature the mountains, valleys, streams and shorelines which make up that country's breathtaking scenery.

In present-day Japan, land is scarce and only the wealthy have large gardens. Otherwise, these are only found in public parks and temple grounds. However, with amazing ingenuity, Japanese gardeners have created exquisite retreats from quite small town plots, reflecting the principles, if not the grandeur, of larger gardens. Outside the Orient, gardeners have incorporated many Japanese ideas into their water gardens, while still retaining the flowers and grass traditionally associated with Western gardens.

Oriental gardens

As early as the beginning of Christianity, Europeans were intrigued by the mysteries of the Orient. In the 13th century Marco Polo brought back fabulous tales of the palaces and gardens of China, and further reports about Chinese art and culture were sent back by Jesuit priests working in Peking. In Europe at that time, gardens were highly stylized, with geometrical shapes dominating the thinking of landscape architects. Chinese gardening, on the other hand, was essentially natural, with every facet designed to be a facsimile of the surrounding countryside. Like landscape painting, gardening in China was thought of as 'shan shui' (mountains and water) and was

closely linked to the other arts of poetry, calligraphy and sculpture. Chinese gardens were rarely seen all at once, but were meant to be discovered scene by scene as the observer strolled from one view to the next. Buildings such as temples, rest rooms and tea rooms harmonized with the environment, being built of natural materials such as bamboo and thatch. These buildings were sited in elevated positions to offer different views of the various features in the garden.

The Chinese and Koreans had such feeling for natural beauty that it is not surprising their near neighbours, the Japanese, were influenced by them. Japanese gardeners first adopted this basic style and then evolved their own, incorporating Shinto and Zen Buddhist teachings into their gardening philosophy.

Contemporary Japanese gardens are monochrome. Mosses, gravel, grasses, shrubs and trees, with their subtle and wide-ranging gradations

Above: *A Japanese public park with the simple harmony of colour and design typical of Oriental gardens.*

Below: *A bridge and waterside irises, Oriental garden features that can be incorporated in the West.*

of green, grey and silver, are all used to great effect. Trees are very important to the scene. They are mostly evergreen, although deciduous maples (*Acer* sp.) are also favoured for autumn colour. Pines and other trees are carefully clipped and trained with wires to give a gnarled weatherbeaten appearance. Pines, in particular, are revered as standing for silence, solitude and old age. Bamboo implies strength and pliability. Peach, plum and cherry trees in blossom herald spring and are held in high esteem. Evergreen azaleas and small-leaved box hedges are clipped and pruned into close rounded shapes to resemble rocks, turtles and tortoises. Irises are used at the edges of pools; otherwise flowers are generally only grown in the garden by 'vulgar and ignorant' people. Bonsai is, of course, another activity involving miniaturization, and Bonsai trees are used extensively in Oriental gardening schemes.

Features of Japanese water gardens

Ancient 'rules' give detailed instructions about the stones and other features of Japanese gardens, including gateways, bamboo fences, walls, pools, lanterns and stepping stones. Lanterns are elaborately classified. They are used at night to light the way for visitors to the tea houses, and to illuminate other garden features, such as bridges.

This use of lanterns is another extraordinary example of Japanese thinking: their gardens are designed to be seen in moonlight, at sunrise, at sunset and in frosty and snowy conditions. Gardens are also planned for the changing seasons, and vantage points are especially designed to enable cherry blossom to be seen at its best. Raked gravel and moss are used instead of grass. This is a positive design feature but also partly due to the severity of winter in many parts of Japan, where grass does not thrive.

Rockwork

The types of stones, their structure, features and correct placement are the most important elements in the design of a Japanese garden and water gardens. Stones which are waterworn are used in water gardens, while rugged rocks are used in mountain scenery. This extensive use of rockwork, often involves the use of huge boulders weighing several tons apiece.

Emulating such design features can cause problems; stone is expensive and even a small piece can weigh a substantial amount. Delivery, offloading and positioning (which often involves a mini-crane) will be charged as extras. But bear in mind that the amount of stone needed will only be proportionate to the size of the pool. If possible, stones should be waterworn. It is also better to use local stone wherever possible, as this will harmonize with the environment. However, the stone must be hard and durable. Remember that the same type of stone may vary greatly. Limestone, for instance, has

Above: *A European public garden created in the Japanese style, beautifully blending water features with a rich and varied planting.*

many forms. From some quarries the stone is hard and will last for years; from others the product is soft and crumbles after the first frost. So, for both aesthetic and economic reasons, local stone scores heavily over the imported variety.

Several types of stone can be used in a water garden. Here are some popular examples:

Limestone is hard and durable. Waterworn varieties are very popular. Colours range from off-white, through buff and grey, to deep red.

Sandstone varies in colour from yellow, through grey-pink, to reddish brown. Being a stratified rock, it is attractive in the garden.

Granite and other igneous and metamorphic rocks are very

Below: *An American University garden with well-positioned rockwork and stone ornaments that reflect the Oriental influence.*

durable. These are often well coloured and sometimes waterworn. Highly recommended.

Slate is stratified and can look very dramatic. Colours range from blue and green to purple.

Tuffa rock is a superb soft rock. It is very porous and soft, providing an ideal home for rockplants and ferns. It is very light in weight but it is relatively expensive.

Water

Japanese pools are normally informal and surrounded by large boulders set firmly in position. Flat areas are incorported to allow easy access for feeding and viewing. These are often paved with flat waterworn stones, with the edges kept in place by cedar logs set in a vertical position. Concrete mouldings of these logs are also frequently used. Trees and bushes are incorporated among the rocks, creating a cool refreshing atmosphere with an air of mystery. Streams are wide but shallow, the bed being filled with stones and boulders to make gushing and gurgling water sounds. The

reflective properties of water are greatly admired, so few aquatic plants such as water lilies and oxygenators are grown. This means that either the stream must be a natural one, or filters must be used to give crystal clear water.

Sand and gravel

The Japanese are fond of using sand or gravel both for pathways and to create special effects. Formerly, sand was used to prevent the feet getting muddy; in later years it was used to signify purity by the Zen masters who developed gardens based on philosophical themes. Sand in the garden today often represents a body of water, and rakes are used to create wave and ripple patterns to heighten the effect. The preferred type of sand has large grains, about 2mm (0.08in) in diameter, and is available in many colours. Mounds of earth or rocks, planted with moss and perhaps dwarf trees, are set amid the sand and gravel, to represent hills and mountains or rocky shorelines.

Stepping stones and pavements

Stepping stones are used both in the water, to enable the owner to cross the pool and so have a better view, and in the grass or moss gardens, to prevent the shoes becoming soiled in wet weather. Sometimes they have a symbolic significance and are carved with words, for example, to indicate the

Below: *A shishi odoshi, a traditional water-driven device originally intended to scare away wild deer.*

seven steps to heaven. Pavements are normally made of natural stone in a form of crazy paving. They are often kept wet by regular spraying to bring out the full beauty of the stone's texture and colour.

Stone ornaments

Stone ornaments traditionally featured in Japanese gardens include lanterns, towers, buddhas and signposts; they are intended to indicate the presence of humanity. By providing light for orientation, directions, or a place in which to worship, they help to make the garden a part of daily life.

Tsukubai and shishi odoshi

Tsukubai are basins containing water for hand washing. These were used before the tea ceremony. A bamboo cup on a long handle and a couple of bamboo sticks for it to rest on are necessary accoutrements.

Shishi odoshi are 'devices' originally developed by farmers for scaring away wild deer and to prevent them from eating the crops. Water is fed through a hollow bamboo pipe into an angled length of thick bamboo. This is set on an axle and has a hollow first joint. Water drips into this cavity, its weight forces the front tip of the bamboo downwards, and the water is released. The pole springs back up and the rear end strikes a small rock carefully positioned behind it, making a sharp, clacking sound. Shishi odoshi are often used at the edge of pools, sometimes as the source of a stream or waterfall.

Streams, waterfalls and bridges

Streams and waterfalls are carefully designed, many types being recognized according to the pattern of water flow they produce. By varying the design, a variety of sounds and visual effects can be produced. Bridges are a popular feature and can be quite elaborate highly-painted wooden structures or simple planks, slabs of stone or curved concrete artifacts. Often, bridges are combined with stepping stones, enabling visitors to cross the pool in several places.

Above: *Carefully positioned stepping stones lead the eye and the foot to a tea house strategically positioned in the subtle depths of a Japanese-style garden. Such ideas give creative food for thought.*

Bamboo fences and gates

The fence is an essential part of the Japanese garden. It ensures privacy and prevents the outside world from intruding. There are many traditional designs in various materials.

Plants for the Japanese garden

We have already mentioned the reasons for using certain plants and trees. Here are tips for growing them successfully.

Bamboo This is a giant grass and certain species grow to enormous proportions in the tropics. In cool temperate countries, however, you will find the hardy, spreading types. Bamboos are evergreen, but can shrivel in winter if they are not given adequate protection from the wind. Plant them on a sun-facing slope if possible, and make sure they are watered and fertilized regularly. Keep them in check by periodically pruning the rhizomes, which tend to stray out of the area designated for them. Propagate them by division.

One of the taller species of bamboo suitable for gardens, *Arundinaria simonii*, spreads quickly by underground runners and can reach a height of 5.5-6m (18-20ft). The leaves may reach a length of 30cm (12in) and a width of 38mm (1.5in). A dwarf species very popular in Japan is *Arundinaria (Sasa) veitchii*. It prefers shade and grows about 1m (39in) tall. It has a yellow stripe running down the edges of the leaves. Excellent for moist soils.

Moss This will grow well in shady moist areas and is commonly used as a ground cover in Japanese gardens. Many species can be collected in woods, but ideally choose the cushion-forming types. Moss gardens must be watered every day in the warmer months if possible. If you wish it to grow on rocks, chop the stems up finely and mix them in buttermilk. Paint the mixture on to the rock face and keep it well watered until it is established.

Azaleas These will only grow in acid to neutral soils – the presence of lime is death to these plants. Plant

Above: *A corner of a Japanese-style garden combining the harmonious sound of falling water with the visual delight of bright azaleas set against a muted background of principally green plants. Waterfalls, classified by design into many categories, are an important theme in Oriental gardening and can form an integral part of a landscaped Koi pond.*

Right: *A show garden incorporating the formal geometry of a gravel bed with the unique artistry of a Bonsai tree positioned to maximum effect.*

them in an ericaceous compost and clip them in late summer after the flowers have faded.

Box The Japanese favour this rather dull shrub because of its ability to tolerate hard pruning. Box (*Buxus* sp.) is an accommodating plant that tolerates lime well; it is thus an ideal substitute for azaleas in chalk or limestone areas.

Pines This group of trees will grow in the poorest soils. The gnarled twisted appearance is achieved by clipping and training.

Bonsai These truly delightful miniaturized trees are freely available in the West, although the prices are somewhat high. It is possible of course to train your own Bonsai and there are plenty of good books available with full instructions on the techniques required.

Western water gardens
Water gardening in the Western hemisphere has developed only over the last few hundred years. It shows a greater diversity than the water gardens found in Japan. The Dutch, French, Italians and the British, for example, have all developed their own styles. The Italians were influenced by Roman and Greek landscape architecture, so their water gardens are mostly very formal, with geometrical shapes and fountains rather than waterfalls. The British borrowed from other styles but have also developed a style of their own. Their water gardens are normally informal, incorporating rock- and bog-gardens, with waterfalls rather than fountains. The British are great plant and flower lovers, so pools tend to be heavily planted with water lilies and other deep marginal plants. They also use many submerged oxygenating plants as well as floating plants. The edges are generally heavily planted with marginals and bog and moisture-loving plants.

For Koi pools, however, planting aquatics is a problem because of the persistent rooting habits of the

41

fish. Oxygenators are quickly uprooted, floating plants are eaten, and the soil from the containers is strewn around the pool, causing an unsightly mess! However, it is still possible to have colour and greenery in a Koi pond, provided that the plants are selected and planted with care.

Water lilies Water lilies – all species or hybrids of *Nymphaea* – are suitable for Koi ponds. Select the most vigorous varieties, such as:

Yellow-flowered: *Nymphaea marliacea chromatella*, 'Moorei', 'Colonel A.J. Welch'.
White-flowered: *Nymphaea alba*, 'Gladstoniana', *Nymphaea marliacea albida*, *Nymphaea odorata alba*.
Pink-flowered: 'Colossea', *Nymphaea marliacea carnea*, 'Masaniello', *tuberosa rosea*.
Red-flowered: 'Attraction', 'Charles de Meurville', 'Conqueror', 'Escarboucle'.

The majority of the water lilies listed above will thrive with up to 120cm (48in) of water above the crown, with the floating leaves spreading

Below: *An informal Koi pond with a strategically positioned Japanese lantern that reflects an Oriental influence in the waterside planting.*

the same distance across the surface of the water. 'Moorei', *marliacea albida*, *odorata alba*, 'Masaniello', and 'Conqueror' are more suitable for 60-90cm (24-36in) water depth.

If you are starting with the tubers, plant them singly in solid tubs, rather than in the planting baskets normally recommended for goldfish ponds. Fill the container with a heavy loam and add a 2.5cm (1in) layer of coarse gravel on the top to stop the fishes stirring up the soil. Firm the tuber well into the container, with just the growing tip showing above the gravel layer.

Position the pots on bricks or other supports to bring them up to the correct water depth for the variety of water lily concerned.

Oxygenators and floating plants
Oxygenating plants, such as Canadian Pond Weed (*Anacharis canadensis*), Willow Moss (*Fontinalis antipyretica*) and *Lagarosiphon* sp., are widely used in ponds because they literally release oxygen into the water in strong sunlight. The problem in Koi ponds is that the larger Koi will quickly destroy such plants and, for this reason, they are not recommended. Another reason for avoiding a lush growth of oxygenating plants (or any green plants for that matter) in a Koi pond

Above: *A simple Oriental-style bridge straddles the 'arm' of an imaginative Koi pond in concrete.*

is that in the absence of light, i.e. during the night, the plants consume oxygen. This may be particularly crucial during warm summer weather, when the low level of dissolved oxygen in the water coincides with a high oxygen demand by the active fishes.

Floating plants will also be destroyed by Koi, although the so-called Water Soldier, *Stratiotes aloides*, will generally survive in a Koi pond, thriving in alkaline water.

Marginal plants
Many varieties of marginal plants, i.e those that thrive in shallow water, are suitable for Koi ponds so long as they are planted in such a way that the Koi cannot uproot them. Either plant them in large tubs or build brick or stone walls along ledges to retain the soil. Supreme among marginal plants are the many varieties of irises that thrive in wet conditions, notably the Laevigatae.

Below: *A well-stocked European Koi pond landscaped with care to suit both Western and Japanese tastes. The pond is butyl rubber.*

PART 2

PLANNING AND BUILDING A POND

In this section, all the theory is put into practice as, having chosen the type, style and position of your pond, you now face the hard work and excitement as it slowly becomes a reality.

As with any large construction task, forward planning is essential; everything must be on hand at the moment it is required, although not everything need be collected together right at the start. Building a concrete/brick pond, for example, takes much longer than putting in a pre-formed pool. Be careful not to rush ahead with ambitious plans without checking some elementary detail: don't hire a machine to dig out a large pond unless you know that you can actually get it round the side of the house to the intended site! Similarly, there is no need to rush out and buy fish and plants at this stage.

For the first-time pond owner, many of the materials and much of the construction work will be completely new; it will pay dividends if each stage is studied carefully and clearly understood before work actually gets under way. This is particularly critical where unfamiliar aquatic equipment is concerned; advance planning where waterfalls and cascades are to be installed is especially important – dismantling a rockery to trace and rejoin a disconnected pipe is no fun.

Perhaps the most important piece of advice of all is to take things at a reasonable pace: for one thing, it will give you time to think and, also, you won't over-tire yourself a few days into what could be a lengthy project – after all, it's not every day the average person is called upon to shift many barrowloads of heavy soil!

Right: *This water feature is already looking good, even though it is yet to be completed.*

44

Pond containers

The pond container is something to hold the water and prevent it from running away or seeping into the surrounding soil. These are available in a variety of materials and shapes, and they can be sunk into the soil to be flush with the soil surface or raised up to form a decorative feature. The cost can vary, depending on the material used and the size. Choosing the material and size will depend very much on your bank balance, your needs and where you wish to put the pond. Ensure that your choice leaves you with a pond that is neither too large for the garden nor too small for the intended fish.

A simple pond will need to have a surface area of at least 1.8m^2 (20ft^2) to support 10 small fishes. Remember that they are going to grow, so that for each 15cm (6in) of fish it is advisable to have 1800cm^2 (2ft^2). To allow not only for the growth of the fishes but also for them to multiply, it is always wise to make a larger pool so that it will cope with its fish population for a number of years. The depth is also important: if it is too shallow, the water will overheat in summer and freeze solid in winter. A deeper pond will allow a wider choice of plants as well as a varied selection of common and exotic fishes.

If you have a formal garden of regular beds and paths, the pond should be rectangular or circular to blend in with the existing arrangement. If, on the other hand, your garden is more natural, with random clumps of planting, meandering paths and a casual layout, then the pond should be as natural as possible, with an irregular shape and looking as if man had no hand in its formation.

With raised ponds where the surface is above ground level, a more formal or regular shape is best; only a rock pool backed by a cliff that cascades its overflow to ground level to be recycled back to the higher pool would look natural. Obviously a raised pond needs a substantial container to prevent the vast weight of water bursting the sides. The advantage of the raised pond is that it allows you to see the fishes and plants and study them closely without stooping.

Below: *Liners to contain water are made either from polythene, PVC which can be reinforced with nylon, or butyl rubber (the most expensive).*

Above: The liner is stretched across the pool cavity and anchored with stones. Water is poured on the liner, which stretches to fill the hole.

Left: A precast pool can be set into the ground by excavating a hole for it to sit in and edging it with slabs.

Above: Pond containers are available in many sizes, shapes and materials.

Types of container

The cheapest form of container uses a plastic liner to contain the water in an excavation. This liner is made of polythene, which breaks down when exposed to sunlight, so it must be shaded between the pool edge and the water level. It has an estimated life of just a year or two, and can only be recommended as a temporary structure. Other liners using plastic have a guaranteed life of three years for the plain and ten years for the laminated varieties; the best quality is the liner made from butyl rubber; this is guaranteed for 15 years but has a life expectancy of over 50 years, and should give a lifetime's use without trouble. With a liner, a pond of almost any shape or size can be made, limited only by your purse and the size of your garden.

Concrete is a wet form of construction that is labour intensive and involves the use of shuttering to contain the concrete until it has cured. Concrete is fine where there is a good solid foundation underneath and the water table is not close to the surface, but where there is a chance of movement it can crack; this will allow the water to seep away, and if the crack is very fine it is difficult to trace for repair.

Precast pools are made from plastic in various weights and in fibreglass. The cost varies and, as in most things, you get what you pay for. The cheapest models are thin and vulnerable to damage; the thicker plastic ones are either semi-rigid or rigid and strong, but more costly; and the most expensive are constructed from fibreglass, which should give a lifetime's use. These pools are fine if the shape and size available happens to meet your requirements.

Should the worst occur and your pool start to leak, there are repair kits that will seal the pool, but usually you will have to empty the water out, store the livestock in a separate container, and replace and balance the water before the livestock can be replaced.

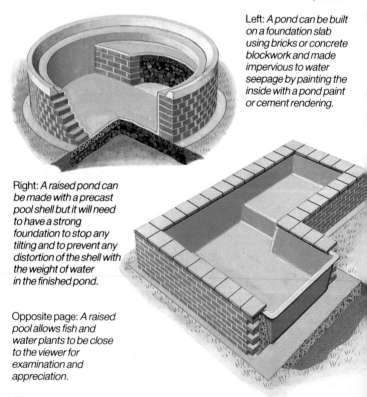

Left: *A pond can be built on a foundation slab using bricks or concrete blockwork and made impervious to water seepage by painting the inside with a pond paint or cement rendering.*

Right: *A raised pond can be made with a precast pool shell but it will need to have a strong foundation to stop any tilting and to prevent any distortion of the shell with the weight of water in the finished pond.*

Opposite page: *A raised pool allows fish and water plants to be close to the viewer for examination and appreciation.*

Installing fountains

Most fountains have the water pump built into them. This has two distinct advantages: first, the weight of the pump base serves as a convenient anchoring device and, second, pipework is either non-existent (the fountain jet normally sits immediately on top of the pump) or, in the case of larger statuary fountains, kept to a minimum. This means that there is negligible friction loss to affect water flow and all the pump's power is fed to the jets.

The basic fountain kit may consist of a pump with jet block attached, although larger models are more likely to have an integral 'T' piece, so that surplus water can be diverted, if required, to an external filtration system or to feed a cascade or waterfall. All fountain kits have a protective sponge-type strainer covering the water inlet to the pump; on some designs this is either extended by additional filter-medium cartridges, or by fitting a much larger extra sponge to act as an efficient filter for the smaller pond. As this strainer becomes clogged, the height of the foundation will diminish – a sure sign that a cleaning session is due!

Depending on size, fountains either operate at full mains voltage or at a safe low voltage; in the latter case, the transformer remains outside the pool, while the fountain/pump unit is in the pond itself. If the pond is a reasonable distance from the house, and you wish to use a low-voltage system, bear in mind that lengthy cable runs may cause a reduction in supply voltage to the pump, lessening jet performance; if this is likely, use low-loss cable. Whatever system is used, a Residual Current Circuit-breaker Device should always be fitted in the electrical supply – water and electricity are bad (often lethal) companions and these fast-tripping circuit-breakers are well worth installing. Similarly, no risks should be taken when laying cable to the pondside; armoured cable should always be used and burying it in plastic pipe adds extra protection against damage from garden forks. Waterproofed junction boxes and switches are also recommended.

Very large, centre-piece fountains can be fed from pumps incorporated in the base in the normal manner, although for very large ponds the use of separate high-power pumps (situated at the pondside) makes maintenance of the pump much easier, unless you are prepared to wade out to the middle, in the event of pump failure.

Siting the fountain needs careful planning. It should be placed so that all the water from the jets falls back into the pond – unless the pond is of a circular, formal design siting a fountain plumb centre will not necessarily achieve this.

Fountains must stand on a level plinth; if not, an asymmetric pattern will be produced. This also applies to centre-piece fountains which feature overflowing cascades from one dish to another, as unlevel siting will result in the water spilling over one side more than the other.

If the overall height of the pump/jet assembly is less than the

Above: *A simple jet complements the classical fountain statue in this formal water garden setting.*

50

pond's water depth, you will need to stand the pump on a couple of bricks, or flat stones, until the jet nozzle just breaks the water surface; bear in mind that large, powerful pumps, such as those used to project geyser-style displays, are liable to topple off their positioning blocks under the influence of their starting-up torque. Large ornamental fountains can also present some problems: they are very heavy and could well cause damage to the pond liner; spread the weight by placing it on flat supporting slabs in the pond, and cushion the supports on expanded polystyrene (styrofoam).

A three-tier jet

Water-bell jet

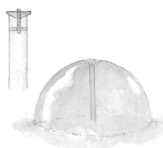

Below: *Position the pump near the pond edge so that you can easily reach the flow-adjuster and inlet strainer. The jet can be mounted on one of the hollow rock-like stands that come complete with convenient ducts for hose feeds.*

Above, left and below: *Just some of the many jet designs that are available from larger suppliers at a wide range of prices. Many have standard fittings that are easy to connect to pumps and some allow adjustment of jet shape or height.*

A water-tulip jet

A fountain jet with separate pump

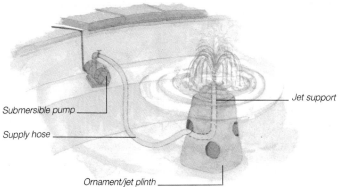

Submersible pump

Supply hose

Ornament/jet plinth

Jet support

Installing cascades and waterfalls

The most important factor to consider when installing watercourses is minimizing water loss. No matter whether the construction involves ready-made units, or is self-designed and built using liner material, rocks and soil, scrupulous attention must be given to ensuring that every drop of water finds its way back into the pond again. Make sure that each preformed unit is level (apart from any tilt necessary to get the water moving in the right direction) and empties directly into the one below. This may seem obvious, but a surprising amount of water can be lost on the way back to the pond; a good insurance policy is to fit a liner beneath the whole cascade to catch any water spillage – a common occurrence, especially with large, splashy water flows. Aquatic plants in the watercourse will also deplete the water supply; although such plants may provide a valuable service in filtering out nitrates from the water, any rampant growth will soon choke the waterway, resulting in unwanted overflows. Algae can also cause water loss, draining it by capillary action into the surrounding soil.

The drawbacks with pre-formed cascade units, especially the less expensive types, are that they are light in weight, and very often rather garish in colour. They will need to be bedded down firmly as they may lift during windy conditions (again resulting in water losses). Glueing sand and grit onto exposed surfaces may help to hide any unnatural coloration and also give some protection against the ultra-violet rays in sunlight that can destroy the plastic. Don't worry too much about the colour of submerged parts as these will soon become disguised with a light coating of natural algae.

During construction, take extra care if rocks are to be included in the design – they will easily puncture the liner material, so the use of protective matting is recommended. Stones or rocks help to interrupt the flow of water

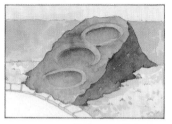

Above: *Ensure that preformed units overlap sufficiently and carry out a trial run before fixing them firmly. Long runs benefit from a liner underneath to catch seepage.*

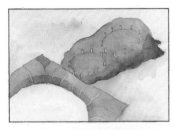

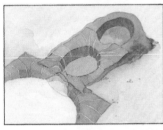

Above: *Start at the base and work up, creating a catchment basin in the main pond. Ensure that sides and lips are firm and that they direct splashes into the pond.*

down a cascade, making its path less predictable, but covering the watercourse base with gravel is not always successful, as the flowing water eventually redistributes it – down to the bottom! Protect any exposed liner material against UV and frost damage by covering it with rocks or soil, and make sure that any overlaps between sections are further waterproofed by applying mastic sealant.

Performance will be impaired if the supply hose from the pump up to the top of the cascade becomes crushed under the weight of a constructed rockery, or is of too small a diameter for the volume of water it is expected to carry. The length of any pipe-run should always be kept to a minimum to reduce friction and optimize pump output power. Water has a knack of getting just where it isn't needed, and it is important that siphonage doesn't occur from, say, the top pool back down through the supply hose and into the bottom pond, via the pump, should the pump be stopped for any reason. Prevent this by keeping the top end of the supply hose above water level at all times.

Waterfalls
Most people associate waterfalls with height, but this need not be excessive to make an effective feature. The sound of gently trickling water is preferable to the roar of a plunging torrent, no matter how much more dramatic the latter looks. Additionally, a straight, falling column of water is rather predictable, whereas a more tortuous path down, say, shallow steps is much more interesting and won't need as much power to operate. If your pond contains fish, another good reason for not having too vigorous a torrent is that it will generally produce too strong a current around the pond, (especially if it is a small one) and will more than likely churn up a continuous cloud of debris and mud as it does so.

Positioning the supply pump at

53

the point of return of a cascade or waterfall will prevent undue turbulence and water currents occurring in small ponds, but this effect may not be so critical in very large ponds.

Where a waterfall is to fall down a rocky face, a more natural effect is obtained if the water doesn't originate right at the top, but emerges from a crevice a little distance down; this also gives you a better chance to hide the end of the supply hose!

The secret of a good waterfall is to make the lipping-stone as smooth and level as possible, so that there is a continuous sheet of water pouring over the edge rather than being concentrated towards one side. In order to maintain the full effect, check that water does not cling to the underside of the lip and so run back out of sight (and possible out of the circulatory system too). Experiment with various contours of stone (or even lipping-pieces of perspex sheeting) until the best effect is achieved. Waterfalls look their best when the falling water remains well clear of any vertical surface behind it; not only does the falling water stay permanently in view but also, by not contacting the vertical rock face, unsightly algae is discouraged from growing.

Waterfalls can be fashioned from almost any material, used in any design – it doesn't have to be over a cliff-face every time. Water gushing from a wall-mounted Lion's head, emerging from an antique crank-handled pump or trickling through a series of upturned roof tiles will provide an attractive focus for your water feature. Very often timber, in the form of old railway sleepers, is used in the construction of waterways; these should be treated to prevent rotting, but take care to use only those sealing agents that do not contain anti-

Above: *Overflowing basins in formal designs such as this need to be mounted absolutely level to prevent lopsided pouring.*

Liner-constructed waterfalls

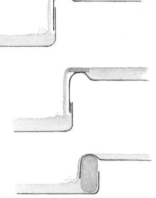

fungal additives. Modern yacht varnish preservatives, for instance, may contain substances to discourage marine animal life (barnacles etc) from attaching themselves to the ship's hull and these may well be toxic to pond fishes over a period of time.

Left: *Use mastic or cement to fill gaps under rocks at the waterfall lip. Overlap liners well, using mastic if required to prevent capillary seepage of water.*

Below: *Changes of direction, as well as changes in level, add interest and can be especially effective in awkward corners.*

Water pumps

Above and left: *Fountains can vary from a small bubble jet to a spray that lifts the water several metres.*

Below: *A non-submersible pump kept in a separate pump house draws the water out of the pond via the pump and returns it to the pool.*

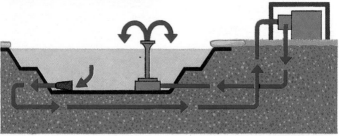

The water pump is the heart of any water movement system, whether it is driving water over a decorative cascade, fountain or waterfall, powering a comprehensive filtration system or even helping to drain the pond. Although here we shall be looking mainly at pond applications, miniature recirculating water pumps are also available for indoor, table-top water-feature ornaments.

Choosing the correct pump for your particular application is critical and it is better to err slightly on the larger side. The performance figures quoted by the pump's manufacturer are calculated under ideal conditions, whereas, when in service, the pump's output may be adversely affected by many new factors: friction losses in long pipe-runs (often of too narrow a bore),

elbows and unions, clogged strainers, extra height demands and ageing of components. If you select a larger pump you can always reduce its output if required. Remember, for fountains you will need a pump capable of supplying pressure, for waterfalls the need is for volume.

Pumps are electrically driven, but there is little danger from electric shock as the components are sealed in, well away from water. Modern pumps feature magnetically coupled, or inductive drives; direct-drive types, with their often vulnerable seals, are not only outdated but also more prone to water damage. There are two types of pump – submersible and surface.

As its name suggests, the submersible type operates under water in the pond itself and needs

Above: *The amount of water that is moved over a waterfall needs a powerful pump.* Below: *A submerged pump lifts the water to top level.*

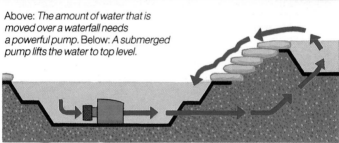

no priming. The pump is cooled by the surrounding water and overheating is rare, but you will need to remove the pump from the pond for maintenance checks and servicing. The majority of submersible pumps operate at full mains voltage but low-voltage models are also available. These are not as powerful, and require a transformer to reduce the mains voltage down to their safe operating level; this may cause a slight complication during installation – there has to be a site near the pool for the transformer. Cable runs from the transformer to the pump should be as short as possible to prevent a drop in voltage occurring.

A surface (or external) pump operates above the water and requires initial priming; a non-return valve in the inlet tube ensures automatic restarting following any interruption in the power supply. Always check that the pump is primed after any stoppage. Surface pumps must be housed in well-ventilated, weatherproof cabinets, which makes servicing a little easier, but they may require more frequent attention (especially in terms of lubrication) than submersible types. Isolating valves are often fitted on either side of the pump to allow for easy, leakproof removal of the unit for servicing.

Strainers, on both the submersible pump and the non-return valve assembly of the surface pump, need very regular cleaning and removal of debris if either type is to continue performing at its best. The larger the strainer, the longer the period can be between cleanings.

When removing a submersible pump from the pond, don't lift it out by pulling on the cable – you may damage the waterproof seal around its exit from the pump body. Both types of pump work best if run continuously, but a yearly inspection, strip-down, lubrication and general service is recommended. This is especially important in hard-water areas, where a build-up of scale in the impeller assembly can cause problems. Before descaling, make sure the descaling agent will not damage any plastic parts.

Of the two types, surface pumps generally have the largest water output, but they can be noisy, and need more plumbing during installation. Submersible pumps are much quieter and less obvious, but they do take up some space in the pond, and the supply cable may be prone to damage and difficult to hide.

Submersible pumps (and the inlet pipe to surface pumps) should be positioned in the pond a little way above the bottom so that detritus is not drawn into the strainer; standing the pump on a brick or two is the best way to do this. Sometimes the inlet (suction) hose feeding a surface pump will collapse under pressure if it is not suitably reinforced, and this can lead to the motor overheating as the impeller is forced to run under dry conditions.

During summer, the action of pumps supplying cascades and waterfalls will help to cool and aerate the pond, but in winter it is better for the pond water to remain less disturbed. To accommodate these differing seasonal demands, position submersible pumps nearer the surface in winter.

It is fairly straightforward to fit extra pipework to any pump to feed an external filter system, a remote cascade, or waterfall, but spirally reinforced hoses of adequate bore must be used to ensure correct water flow and to prevent crushing when buried. Normal garden hose is not suitable, and clear PVC hose (often

prone to premature ageing, inflexibility and kinking) soon gathers an internal coating of algae under the influence of light; choose a suitably coloured hose.

A submersible pump can be incorporated exclusively into a biological filter system, rather than driving a fountain; details of this process, together with plumbing plans can be found on pages 80 and 86-87.

In Koi ponds with external gravity-fed filters, there is a subtle difference in usage between surface and submersible pumps. Submersible types should be positioned at the output end of the filter (thus 'pulling' the water through the system), while surface pumps are set at the front of the filter, 'pushing' the water through. In either case, the pumps should be situated as low as possible to maintain maximum pressure at the inlet. The normal water through-put in Koi ponds is usually much higher than is recommended for goldfish-stocked, planted ponds, and very often central-heating system pumps are pressed into service for the purpose.

Above: *Submersible pumps are readily available, easy to install and often come complete with 'T' piece, flow-adjuster and jet.*

Right: *You will need to look closely to see the water returning to this pond. Its corner site makes it unobtrusive yet accessible.*

A direct-drive pump

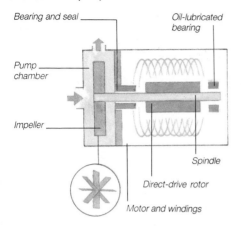

Bearing and seal

Oil-lubricated bearing

Pump chamber

Impeller

Spindle

Direct-drive rotor

Motor and windings

Left: *The main shaft runs through a seal and bearing directly to the motor, giving a powerful output, but wear on the seal can eventually let water into the motor.*

An induction-drive pump

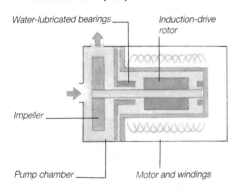

Water-lubricated bearings

Induction-drive rotor

Impeller

Pump chamber

Motor and windings

Left: *Indirect-drive and water-lubricated bearings reduce the torque of the pump, but by avoiding the need for seals, reliability is often improved.*

Electricity in the garden

The combination of electricity and water can be lethal, particularly when a human being joins the two together, but if protected properly it is perfectly safe. The first rule is to make sure that all electrical equipment that is bought has been expressly made for outdoor use, and that all instructions, no matter how silly or inappropriate they may seem, are followed to the letter. The second rule is to keep it in good repair and well maintained. Where cables have to be used in the garden – especially if they are to be buried under flower beds – use an armoured cable (one that is covered with toughened plastic or metal). All switches and junction boxes must be completely waterproof.

If in any doubt about your system, call in a qualified electrician to advise you. Secure all cables so that they will not cause any hazard; avoid draping wires along a flimsy fence that could be blown down in a severe gale, and keep them out of hedges or shrubs that are likely to be clipped or pruned. If you decide to run the cable under ground, bury it deeper than 45cm (18in) to prevent a garden spade inadvertently severing it. Also make sure that the cable route is clearly

marked: you might remember where it runs, but if the house is sold the new occupiers need to know where the cable is to avoid trouble. A plastic strip is available to warn of buried cables. All this may sound too much trouble, but it is vitally important.

Safety measures

It is not always necessary to have full mains electricity to run pool equipment. The current can be stepped down through a transformer to a lower AC voltage or to very low DC voltage provided the equipment is suitable. If an accident occurs, the

Above: *The enjoyment of the garden can be extended after dark by using electricity to power lights and the pump that moves water in the pool.*

shock would then be well within safety limits and cause no harm.

As a safety precaution, all outside mains circuits should be fitted with a circuit breaker so that if there is any leakage of current the circuit breaker automatically switches off the power. Choose a model that is suitable for personal protection, rated at 30 milliamps, and takes no more than 30 milliseconds to trip. This will ensure

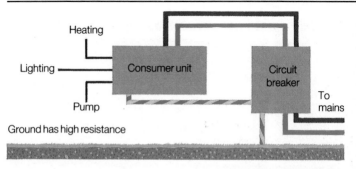

Heating

Lighting

Consumer unit

Circuit breaker

Pump

To mains

Ground has high resistance

Above: *Position the circuit breaker between the consumer unit and the main fuse to give full protection.*

that if someone touches a live wire or a live section of a piece of equipment, then the instant the current starts to run through the person it will switch

Below: *There is a wide variety of lights that are made for outdoor use and are highly suitable for the garden. Some are constructed to work under water with a choice of colour filters. Lights can be permanently fixed or portable, giving spots or general illumination.*

off before any damage is caused and the person will be unharmed. There are various models of circuit breaker; they can be wired into the electrical circuit at the fuse box, or they can be wired in as a power socket or as part of a plug. The plug will cover only one appliance, but the socket, provided it has an adaptor, can service more than one item, and the circuit controller will cover all the machines on the whole circuit.

Lighting and heating
Electricity is not only for pumps but also covers lighting and heating. Here

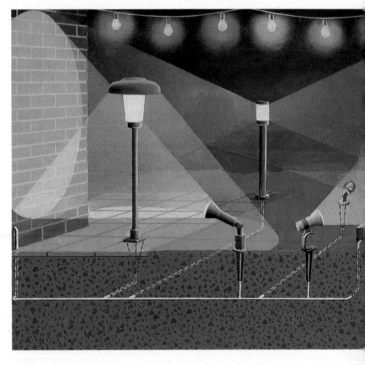

again it is important to use the right equipment – lights that have been designed specially for exterior use, either as individual lights or as strings of bulbs for illuminating the garden. Some lights for the pond are used floating or submerged, sometimes attached to a fountain to give a variety of colours to the spray. Most lighting comes in either flood or spot models: the flood will illuminate a wide area, whereas the spot throws a concentrated beam onto one feature, and gives a more dramatic effect. Where light is required to illuminate a hazard such as steps it is better to use a flood, which has a more overall light, rather than a spot, which can cause confusing shadows.

The low-powered lighting circuits that are available in kits complete with transformer allow the user to clip the lights directly into the cable, which is covered with a self-sealing plastic so that when the light is removed the cable becomes weatherproof again. The light can be placed anywhere along the length of cable without complicated cable stripping.

Where lighting cables are strung overhead it is necessary to support the wire with an additional stout galvanized wire secured to it with clips. Insulating tape is a short-term method that will rot after a year or two, leaving the cable unsupported. Plastic plant ties or clips will last much longer and hold the cable securely. A combination of both tape and ties is even better, as the tape will prevent any chafing.

Electricity provides a very convenient and easy form of power that gives light, drives motors and provides heating – the last is very useful when the pool becomes frozen in winter. Floating a special heater will keep a small area of the pool clear of ice; the fishes will benefit from the oxygen intake, and it will prevent the build-up of noxious gases under the ice. Sophisticated systems can be constructed using a thermostat so that the current is switched on automatically when the temperature drops below freezing and off again when it rises; this cuts down the current used to keep the pond clear.

Using a plastic liner

Place the pond out in the open where possible; this will encourage good plant growth. Allow plenty of space around it for access to the fish and plants. Mark out the area needed and then check the levels; it is very rare to find a garden that is absolutely flat, even if it looks level. The pool structure must lie level and the spoil dug out can be used to build up a ridge to make the liner just contain the water and not stick up at one end.

When digging the pond it is important to incorporate shelves along the sides, at least 20cm (8in) wide and 23cm (9in) below the water surface, to accommodate plants that need just a little water over their roots. The deeper parts can be dug to a depth suitable for your plants and fishes: this should be not less than 45cm (18in) deep. Deeper ponds are needed for Koi, which need water about 1.5m (5ft) deep. Shallow ponds are prone to freezing in winter and overheating in summer, to the distress of the fishes. Remove a strip of turf around the edge, about 5cm (2in) deep and 45cm (18in) wide, for the liner to bed into.

The liner should be plenty large enough and the size can be calculated by taking the overall dimensions and adding double the

depth to the length and double the depth to the width. For example, if the hole measures 3.6m (12ft) long, 2.4m (8ft) wide and 60cm (2ft) deep, then the liner should be 3.6m (12ft) plus twice the depth of 60cm (2ft) long and 2.4m (8ft) plus twice the depth of 60cm (2ft) wide, so the pool requires a liner 4.8m (16ft) by 3.6m (12ft).

The liner needs to be pulled fairly taut across the pool and anchored round the edge with heavy weights such as paving slabs. Water is then poured into the liner, which will stretch with the weight and start to conform to the profiles of the cavity, becoming more tight to the walls as the water reaches the top. The liner edge can be trimmed of excess material to leave some 30-45cm (12-18in) to be covered with turf or paving slabs; the latter can be bedded in a generous layer of mortar.

Below: *Mark out the pool shape with pegs and string, check the levels, then start the excavation. Line the hole with a layer of sand to give a smooth surface; then stretch the liner over, anchoring the edges with stones. Next, pour in the water, which stretches the liner to fit the hole's contours. Finally, trim the edges and cover with stones or turf.*

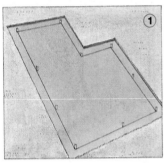

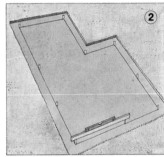

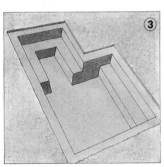

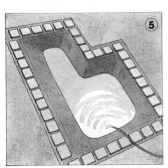

Using a precast shell

Positioning a precast pond is best achieved by inverting the shell and laying it on the ground in the right place and marking its exact outline, but this is unfortunately suitable only for symmetrical pools. Irregular ones have to be placed right way up, and the edge marked by dropping vertical positions to the ground. Check the levels to allow for any building-up of soil around one end, otherwise you may have one end of the precast shell sticking out of the ground.

When a precast pond has to be set into the soil it is necessary to dig a hole to conform as closely to the shell as possible. This is quite an undertaking, particularly if the shell is large, and when the hole is completed there are usually some gaps around the edge that need to be back-filled. This is done with sand, ramming it well down to give the cast as much support as possible. There are difficulties where the gaps are under the planting shelves or the shell's base; but if a layer of sand is spread on these flat surfaces and the cast wriggled into position, the sand will conform closely to the shape of the shell. Awkward areas are sometimes filled with sand by forcing down the sand with a jet of water from a hosepipe, which will wash the sand into the cavities that otherwise cannot be reached.

Once the precast pond is in position and the edges again checked for levels it can be filled with water, which will make it settle a little. A semi-rigid pool cast will have its sides pressed out against the walls of the hole, but the fibreglass models are more rigid and will be more inflexible. Some ponds have the edge built into the cast and can be left exposed, whereas others need a covering to make them a little more unobtrusive. This can be done using turf, stone or paving slabs, though the latter need to be bedded onto a layer of mortar for stability. Remember to leave the water to settle for a reasonable length of time, so that it can reach the temperature of its surroundings and lose the chlorine and other harmful gases. Only then should you set about introducing plants and fishes into the pond.

Above: *A pond similar to this can be constructed using a precast shell. The shell is initially placed upside down in its intended position and*

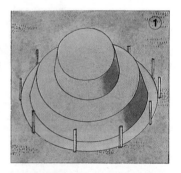

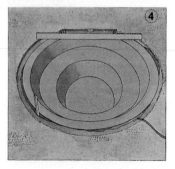

marked with pegs. The hole is then excavated to conform as closely as possible to the shell, which is placed in the hole and any gaps are packed with sand. The levels are checked and the pool filled with water; the edge can be trimmed with paving slabs or stones for a neat effect.

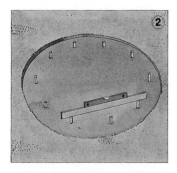

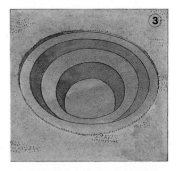

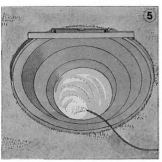

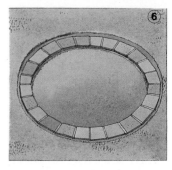

A raised precast pond

A raised pond needs a substantial foundation under the cast to prevent the pond tilting or sinking, and plenty of reserve strength around it to contain the weight and stop the shell distorting and splitting. After placing the shell in position, carefully measure the height of the pond and mark it with canes and string so that you can be satisfied with the overall positioning. Remove the top soil, spread a 10cm (4in) layer of hardcore over the site and firm it down well. Place a further 10cm (4in) of concrete over the top and smooth off.

If the overall dimensions are in excess of 2.4m (8ft) in either direction

it is wise to include some steel reinforcing. This can be welded mesh or a grid of rods wired together to form 10-15cm (4-6in) squares. Large ponds should have the thickness of concrete increased to 15cm (6in) to give a stable base, and this thickness

Below: *Place the casting in position and mark off with pegs; remove the top soil and lay a foundation slab on top of hardcore. The shell is then replaced and the perimeter wall is built backfilling with concrete; as this proceeds, the pool is filled with water. Finally, the top is finished with slabs. Allow to settle before planting.*

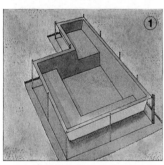

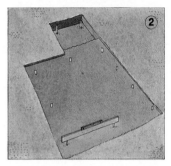

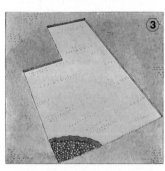

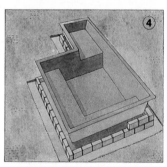

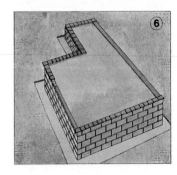

should also be used where the soil is soft or unstable, whatever the size.

The cast can be set onto the concrete if both surfaces are smooth, but if either is irregular then a bed of mortar should be spread for the shell to be vibrated into place; check the levels in both directions. The perimeter wall needs a foundation similar to the pond base, with the hardcore finishing some 45cm (18in) below ground level and 45cm (18in) wide to provide adequate support for a wall of 23cm (9in) thickness.

The wall can be constructed of brick, concrete block or stone to fit into the garden scheme. As it rises a weak mixture of concrete of eight parts of ballast to one of cement can be packed between the wall and the cast; the concrete should be only just moist. If the cast appears too flexible it can be part filled with water to compensate for the exterior pressure.

Continue the wall and back-filling until level with the top of the cast, and smooth off to give a fine finish on the top surface. An alternative is to cover the top with stone or tiles, which should be set into a mortar bed and pointed between the stones or tiles to give a frost-proof finish. The pond should be filled with water and allowed to settle before planting.

Using concrete

Mark out with pegs the area to be covered by the pond. Check the levels with a spirit level to make sure that the whole structure will be set into the ground without any section projecting above the surface; if this is likely to happen, some additional soil should be used to build up the space to cover the concrete. The hole should be dug out allowing for the thickness of the walls and base, which depends on the shape, depth and size of the pond. Unless you are constructing the pond in solid rock you should allow at least 10cm (4in) thickness for a small pond and 15cm (6in) for a larger one.

Where possible incorporate some reinforcing material: chicken wire is suitable for small ponds, but larger ones need reinforcing with something more substantial, and the fairly complicated large ponds with several levels really require the services and expertise of a fully qualified structural engineer to work out the stresses. This is very important, for even a small pond can hold several tons of water.

Having excavated the hole, check it again for the levels. Prepare the reinforcing and spread the concrete over the base, adding the reinforcing where necessary. The whole is tamped down, to squeeze out any air bubbles, and then allowed to mature for a day or so. The shuttering for the walls is placed into position; this is substantial boarding to hold the wet and plastic concrete in place until it is dry. The concrete is poured into this mould in one action, vibrated to allow air bubbles to escape, and left to set. The shuttering can then be removed, and the base and walls covered with a slurry of sharp sand and cement rubbed well into the surface and allowed to dry thoroughly.

Fill the pond with water, and leave it for a day or two to absorb the chemicals from the cement, then pump it out and refill, and repeat this several times. An alternative is to treat the surface with a proprietary sealing product that will save all the filling and unfilling; water is then poured in and left to mature. Allow the natural and added chemicals to disperse before you introduce any plants or fishes. This will prevent problems later on.

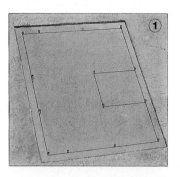

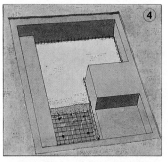

Above: *Mark out the pond position with pegs and string, check the levels, and then dig out the hole. To lay a suitable concrete foundation slab*

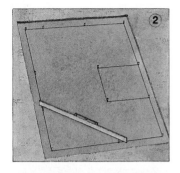

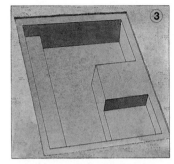

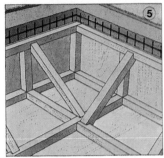

incorporating some reinforcing metal, put up some shuttering to hold the wet concrete sides in position; place in the reinforcement before pouring

and vibrating the concrete. Remove the shuttering when the concrete is dry and paint the sides with a pool paint to contain the chemicals.

Pond edging

We have seen that with the 'natural' pond the dividing line between water and land tends to be quite indistinct, even imperceptible at times. In many garden ponds, edging is far more clearly established.

With liner ponds, any liner material above the water level is exposed to both summer sunlight and winter frosts, both damaging influences on less-expensive materials. Shading with any form of overhanging edging will provide necessary protection. However, overhanging edging can prevent wildlife leaving the pond, and allow easier access to cats and to young children. Of course, each slab that projects out over the water must have the greater part of its area firmly anchored to prevent tilting.

In addition to 'finishing off' the pond, the surround can serve as a functional device: a low brick wall not only holds back earth from the pond, but also acts as a physical safety barrier to children. Constructions like this can appear too stark – plants set against them will help to soften the often unavoidable straight lines. Any exposed brickwork and mortar that is likely to come in contact with the pond water should be sealed with the appropriate compound before water and fish are added.

When designing the pond's edging, the materials should be selected to harmonize with any other nearby structures – stone paths, walls etc. Even where no edging is present, and the lawn extends right to the water's edge, a certain amount of constructional planning is necessary to maintain a firm edge and to prevent soil (and fertilizers or pesticides) from entering the water. A small pebble-filled drainage channel beneath the turf should be incorporated right around the pond's perimeter. Make sure that the drainage direction is away from the pool.

Different types of surround are installed at different stages of pond construction. For a brick wall of any reasonable dimensions, a foundation collar of concrete should be laid down (and allowed to set) *well before* the pond itself is excavated; on the other hand, a decorative edging of bricks can, with liner ponds, be set in a cement-mortar bed, level with the surrounding earth, after the liner is installed. Whatever material is used, a pond's surround must be perfectly level – there is nothing worse than viewing a widening expanse of liner from the other side of the pond. Safety is obviously essential where the pondside is likely to attract a considerable amount of 'traffic' and any paving must be set down firmly, and, more important, perfectly evenly. Once away from the edge proper, however, any surround can be allowed to slope gently away from the water if so desired; this will prevent rain from washing dirt into the pond, and, on icy days, anyone sliding in! Remember, when planning permanent surrounds, to allow gaps or entry points for such things as cables and pipework.

Stones and rocks make excellent pond banks, but again take care during installation. Make sure the heaviest stones are firmly supported from beneath the liner, by a concrete 'plank' if necessary, and protect the liner from damage by the stone with a sandwich layer of matting; don't forget that stones toppling into the water can also damage the liner, so avoid using soft stones that may disintegrate under the influence of rain or returning cascade water. Soft stone is also best avoided as many soluble rocks can contain minerals that adversely affect the pond's water quality.

To create a beach effect, leave a much wider area of liner around the pond to allow for the very gradual reduction in water depth necessary to stop stones sliding. It may be necessary to fix the top layers of pebbles in position with blobs of aquarium sealant (safer than cement or mortar) to prevent them shifting under paddling feet, or being thrown into the pond (both favourite occupations of children).

Edging with paving slabs

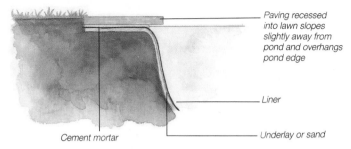

Paving recessed into lawn slopes slightly away from pond and overhangs pond edge

Liner

Cement mortar

Underlay or sand

Edging with turf

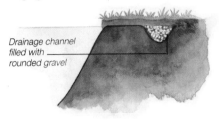

Drainage channel filled with rounded gravel

Above: *Recess paved edging into turf, bedding it on cement mortar. Remember to leave room for cables and hose.*

Left: *Turf is a very natural form of edging. A drainage channel filled with gravel will reduce muddying.*

Edging with boulders

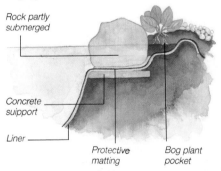

Rock partly submerged

Concrete support

Liner

Protective matting

Bog plant pocket

Left: *For another natural effect, partly submerge boulders around the pond edge. Flap the liner up behind to form a pocket for bog plants.*

Below: *Pondside bog areas are easier to maintain than ones in the pond ones. Make sure that excavation does not weaken pond walls.*

Bog areas beside the pool

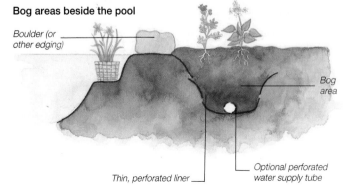

Boulder (or other edging)

Bog area

Thin, perforated liner

Optional perforated water supply tube

Constructions in the pond

There are obvious objects that can be constructed in the garden pond, such as islands and bridges; but there are also less obvious items such as decks, jetties, stepping stones, waterfalls, and bases for sculpture and fountains that border or intrude into the water area. These can be a problem when it comes to placing them into position. The most important problem is how to put them into place without upsetting, breaking or damaging the pond structure, whether it is concrete, plastic liner or a precast shell. If there is an adequate concrete base under the pond, there should be no problem; and of course it is better to think of this element before the pond is constructed, in order to make allowances in the foundation work, and add extra strength where there is to be extra weight. But if you inherit a pond or have a sudden desire to add to your own construction, it will entail certain precautions for success.

The best method, when you have a heavy weight that has to rest on something rather fragile, is to spread the load over a wide area; this means making the foundation cover as wide a space as possible. If you have a pond liner and you wish to build a pier to support a bridge, fountain or stepping stone, place a large flat stone (or even a couple of paving slabs) on the flat base of the pond to carry the weight. If the slab has sharp edges and corners these should be cushioned with a double layer of pond liner – a piece of the original liner that was trimmed off when it was being constructed will be sufficient. Upon this flat slab the structure can be built up with confidence.

If the pond is in use, remember that any cement or concrete work will give off free lime into the water, which can damage the livestock. All work should be treated with a suitable pond paint to isolate new cement work. To keep structures as light as possible, use hollow blocks and build with plenty of holes in the construction.

Where there is an undulating base that does not allow a paving slab to bed flat on the base, a layer of sand can fill out the hollows and give the slab something to setle down on. This

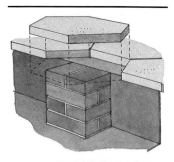

Above: *It is necessary to build a pier to support a hexagonal paving slab that projects over the pool edge.*

Below: *Stepping stones can be made on top of a pool liner by spreading the weight over a larger area using paving slabs. All concrete materials have to be painted with pond paint to seal in the chemicals. Hollow blocks can be filled using plastic bags of concrete.*

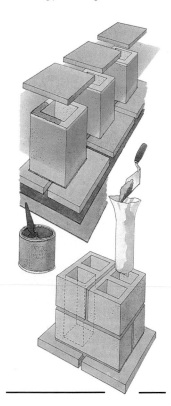

Above: *A bridge adds beauty to this pool.*

Left: *When building a pier or jetty on a sloping base it is necessary to provide a concrete foundation under the liner to support the weight evenly.*

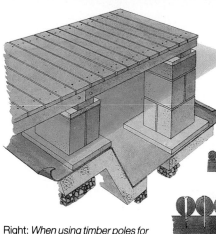

Right: *When using timber poles for constructions, they can be either fixed with nails, screws or bolts, or wired together using heavy duty staples into the main timbers.*

Right: *An island can be made in a pool even when using a liner. It should be distinguished as a shape in the excavation, so the liner is stretched over it when filled with water. The edge of the island is secured with slabs and the plastic cut to expose the soil which can then be planted.*

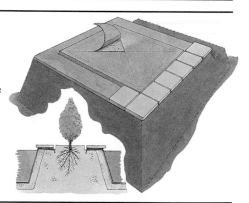

will not work on a sloping base, where it is usually necessary to build up a foundation of wet concrete; this invariably means draining the pond to make a good job.

Constructing an island is a simple matter when the pond is originally being built with a liner; leave the soil in position and stretch the liner over it, anchor it and trim the edges as the ordinary pond edge. Where there is an existing pond, it is best to build a wall of brick or stone and infill with soil to make an island.

Timber can be used, but make sure that any wood preservative that has been used is suitable for the pond and livestock. If the timber has weathered well it can be used, but if in doubt cover the timber in a seal such as

yacht varnish and allow it to dry thoroughly before placing it in the water. Bridges need to be safe: it is no pleasure to be suddenly dropped into cold water, either by the collapse of the structure or by slipping on a mossy surface. Check that there is adequate strength in the structure, as people like to congregate on a bridge to look at the water and livestock. Railings need to be more than adequate and securely fixed to the whole structure.

Waterfalls and cascades should be built so that no water can escape through leaks, particularly where there are overlaps in the construction. Liners work very well in this sort of structure, being discrete in appearance yet thoroughly reliable.

Below: *To place a pump in shallow water it is necessary to construct a sump to conceal it; the cover can be made from loose-laid paving slabs.*

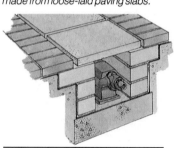

Below: *When using railway sleepers as pool sides it is important to lay the pool liner behind them to render the whole structure waterproof.*

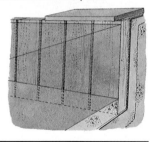

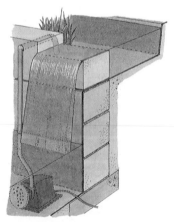

Left and below: *When constructing waterfalls it is important to keep the whole stream contained in a waterproof channel, making sure that liners are used effectively and no leakage occurs. Conceal all piping behind the stonework or planting.*

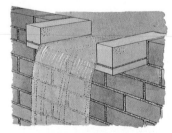

Above: *An edging of pebbles in a pond can look very sympathetic.*

Right: *When constructing a beach of pebbles it is necessary to provide a container to stop them from rolling down to a lower level. This is achieved by building a raised, rigid section under the pool liner.*

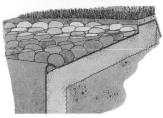

Below: *The use of an old pump head can be most effective as a fountain head, seen here secured to an old railway sleeper as a support.*

Below: *The pump lies below the water surface, where it forces the water up to issue from the pump, and to drop back down and be recycled again.*

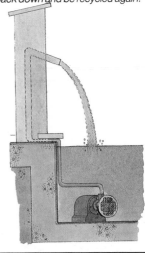

Water quality

To most people water is a simple liquid with a chemical basis of two hydrogen atoms combining with one of oxygen; but in nature it can vary considerably, as natural water contains other chemicals and organisms that can change its properties. Those waters with a high lime content are referred to as hard water, whereas low lime waters are referred to as soft. This is due to rain falling on soils that have a high or low lime content and picking up minerals as they filter through the layers of soil. Near volcanic vents, the minerals saturate the water to produce very unpalatable waters rich in sulphur or magnesium.

Tap water may also have other additions; chlorine and fluoride are probably the two best known, but even in soft-water areas some authorities add lime to make the water less acid. Rain water can present problems if you live to the windward of certain factories that emit fumes with a high sulphur content; these fumes can combine with water vapour in the air to form sulphuric acid and cause what is known as 'acid rain', which has cleared lakes in Scandinavia of fishes and plant life, leaving the water a clear blue but totally devoid of life.

The quality of pond water

If you want to keep fishes, water is a vital factor, and it must be able to support life without causing suffering. To use tap water, it is necessary to allow the chlorine to disperse, which it will do if left for a week or so, before any plants or fishes are introduced into the pond. Unlike chlorine, the more complex chloramines (added at water treatment stations) have to be removed by using ammonia-adsorbing materials, such as zeolite or activated carbon, in the pond's filter system. Proprietary additives are available to speed up the maturation process in new ponds, but to use these successfully you need to know how much water the pond holds. Calculating this can be tricky, especially with irregularly shaped ponds, but elementary mathematics is all that is needed

Above: *The sea evaporates to form clouds of water vapour that fall on cooler high ground as rain.*

Above: *By testing the water, the acidity or alkalinity can be determined and balanced as needed.*

with rectangular ponds. Multiply length by width by depth in centimetres and divide by 1,000 for metric volume (litres). If you are using imperial measurements (feet), multiply by 6.23 to give Imperial Gallons (4.5 litres); the US gallon is slightly smaller and is equal to 0.83 Imp. gallon or 3.78 litres.

A simple test is to watch the health of the plants and fishes: if they thrive, the water is reasonably balanced; but if the fishes become a poor colour, show no sign of growth and move sluggishly, then the water is suspect.

There are various forms of testing kits available that have been developed for aquarium use, swimming pools and soil testing, and these can be used to register the chemical level and the balance of acidity and alkalinity of the water. You can check for any deterioration in water quality by periodically testing for nitrite (NO_2) and pH (acidity/alkalinity). Test kits are very easy to use; they are both reliable

Above: *A waterfall is an ideal way to increase the oxygen level in the water, helping both fish and plants.*

and accurate and latest methods of packaging the test strips or dry reagents ensure that there is little variation in results even with ageing. (Kits are also available for testing water for oxygen, hardness, ammonia, copper and numerous other substances, but you may require some aquatic experience to interpret their results.)

In the event of any drastic changes occurring, you should always investigate the causes before taking suitable remedial measures. High levels of nitrites and nitrates often caused by overfeeding or poor pond hygiene management can be reduced by a partial water change (although nitrate may well be present in the domestic water supply to start with). Changes in pH may be due to dead fish, or perhaps to pollutants that may have been introduced unwittingly into the pond; again a partial water change will bring relief. It is important that you make any deliberate alterations in pH very slowly over a period of time so as not to stress the fish.

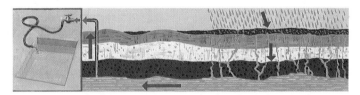

Above: *The mineral content of tap water is determined by the soils that the rain has filtered through.*

Below: *The chemicals emitted by factories can combine with water vapour in the air to form acid rain.*

If water is left static, without stirring or being moved, it becomes stagnant. The mineral salts in the water act together with sunlight and encourage the primitive plant life called algae and the proliferation of free-swimming green organisms, which make the water look green; eventually they die and start to putrify, using up oxygen and producing toxic gases. On the other hand, if the water is partially shaded to keep out some of the sunlight (usually by growing plants that will cover some of the surface), and organisms added that compete with or eat the algae and green organisms, the algae will be kept to a permissible level.

An electric pump is normally used to force the water to a higher level, so that it returns naturally to its original level over a waterfall. Alternatively, it can be ejected into the air through a fountain nozzle. These methods both cause the water to break up into droplets, which have a large surface area and can pick up more oxygen; this oxygen-enriched water is excellent for supporting pond life.

Contamination of the water
Avoid making the water too rich in nutrients by feeding the aquatic plants with ordinary fertilizers, manure or humus, as this will encourage the growth of algae; instead, keep to those fertilizers made exclusively for aquatic use.

Another problem that can occur is the draining into the pool of water from surrounding areas of grass and vegetation, bringing with it chemicals that have been used as fertilizers, or for killing pests, diseases or plants. Depending on the nature of these chemicals, the water can cause either temporary or permanent damage. Most modern chemicals are checked for toxicity and are passed for domestic use only if they have been proved perfectly safe when used as instructed. However, old chemical sprays and treatments are still available that can cause pollution in the garden pool. Where possible make sure that any natural drainage into the pond is diverted to drain away in a place where damage will not occur. When using sprays try to ensure that the fine droplets are not

THE EFFECTS OF HIGH ACIDITY AND ALKALINITY

Ponds that are too alkaline
Alkaline conditions are a common problem in ponds, especially newer ponds, and if the pH of your water is regularly over 8.5, conditions will become stressful to fish and other pond life. pH values above 9 signal a serious problem, especially if excessive growths of algae are not the cause, and you will need to rapidly remedy the situation.

Symptoms of high pH
• Fish become prone to fungal and other diseases as their mucus coating is damaged.
• Waste products (ammonia) in the water become more toxic.
• Fish gills may be damaged, and fish die without showing any external systems.
• Plant growth will be less lush

and oxygenating plants may have a powdery coating of off-white calcium on their leaves.
• Biological pond filters will fail to work as effectively.

Ponds that are too acid
Acid conditions are less common than alkaline ones in ponds, but when they occur, fish and other water life can become stressed.

Symptoms of low pH
• Fish become more prone to disease, they may have reddened fins, and they may die for no apparent reason, without showing any external symptoms.
• Some pond plants, particularly oxygenators, will not grow well in acid conditions.
• Biological pond filters will fail to work as effectively.

carried by the wind into the pond.

Apart from the external influences which may contaminate the pond water, the main contributory factor to deteriorating water quality is, of course, the animals and plants living in the water itself – assisted by the over-generous pondkeeper who overfeeds (while probably maintaining that it's in the best interests of the fish). The continual production of waste matter by the fishes, together with seasonal decaying plant material and uneaten food, leads to a build-up of toxic ammonia-based substances. These, if not removed from the pond (or if their damaging effects are not neutralized by some other means), will eventually cause water quality problems no matter how large the pond.

Keeping the water clean

While the aquarium-keeper can help to keep dissolved (and consequently unseen) toxins down to a reasonable level by partial water changes, the pondkeeper must turn to other more practicable (and less labour-intensive) means of keeping the water pure.

Toxic nitrogenous compounds can also be reduced by a bioligical filter system; this uses colonies of nitrifying bacteria to change them first to nitrites and then to nitrates. (More details of this system of filtration can be found on pages 80, 86 and 87.) Modern external filter systems equipped with foam sponge filter-media and ultra-violet water-sterilizing lamps not only remove debris, act biologically and kill bacteria, but have also proved effective against green water. (Though paradoxically, the use of a really efficient filter may even increase growth of some other types of algae – Blanketweed – in the pond by allowing light to penetrate deeper into the now crystal-clear water.)

Below: *New ponds are particularly vulnerable to algal bloom. Green water is the result of an abundance of nitrates in the water, and algal growth is encouraged by light and warmth. Avoid overfeeding fish and using ordinary plant fertilizers.*

Filters and aeration systems

A pond ecosystem can be self-sustaining if it is well stocked with plants, has a balanced number of fishes and receives adequate sunlight. However, the persistent 'rooting' habit of Koi allows few plants to survive, and thus to maintain good water quality the Koi-keeper will need to install a filter, pump and aeration system. In this section, we look at the different filter types in general, and then consider the installation of suitable aeration systems in a pond.

Filtration processes

Filtration is the process by which debris is removed from the water, while at the same time organic waste products are converted into less harmful substances. There are three basic methods of filtration: mechanical, chemical, and biological. Often more than one of these methods is in operation at the same time in any particular filter system.

Mechanical filtration This is simply the mechanical removal of solid detritus as the water passes through a suitable medium, such as gravel, sponge or synthetic fibres. The trapped solids are then removed from the system, either by back-flushing into a drain or by taking out the filter material for cleaning or replacement.

Chemical filtration In this case the filter medium exerts a chemical influence on the water as it passes through. Commonly used chemical filter media include zeolite and activated carbon, which will extract organic wastes, inorganic chemicals and carbon dioxide from the water.

Biological filtration As the name implies, this method of filtration makes use of natural biological processes to purify the water. Although they vary in design, all biological filters support a colony of aerobic bacteria (i.e. those that flourish in oxygen-rich conditions) that convert toxic ammonia produced by the decomposition of

organic wastes into progressively less harmful substances that are then recycled in the so-called 'nitrogen cycle'.

The principal so-called nitrifying bacteria involved are *Nitrobacter* sp., which convert ammonia (NH_3) to nitrites (NO_2), and *Nitrosomonas* sp., which convert nitrites to nitrates (NO_3). In a well-balanced system, the nitrates are absorbed by growing plants as a fertilizer and the plant protein then becomes a food source for the animals within the pond, thus completing the cycle.

Filter media

Before we look at the working principles of various filters, we review the common filter media and their characteristics.

Processed lava granules The sponge-like formation of these granules gives them a high surface area-to-volume ratio: they are covered with crevices on the outside and have a matrix of capillaries on the inside. Because of its structure, this material is a very efficient physical filter. It also encourages biological filtration because it provides a large surface on which beneficial bacterial colonies can form. It is inert, sterile, neutral in pH and very light, with a dry density of about $500kg/m^3$ (approximately $40lbs/ft^3$).

Baked clay granules These lightweight spherical granules are favoured by many filter manufacturers. They are also used for hydroculture, i.e. growing plants in a fertilized solution with the granules acting as an inert support.

Gravel This is available in several grades; the coarser grades of about 6mm (0.25in) particle size are probably the best. Canterbury Spar is a much favoured gravel medium because the irregular shape and porous nature of the particles provide a large surface area as a haven for beneficial bacteria, as well as producing good mechanical straining properties. A particle size of 6-10mm (0.25-0.4in) is ideal.

Sand This can only be used in sand pressure filters, because it clogs quickly and needs frequent back-flushing – a difficult procedure with many gravity-fed filters. (See under 'Sand pressure filters', page 88).

Foam Foam can act as both a mechanical and biological filter, but it has a tendency to clog and therefore needs frequent cleaning. There are many types of sheet foam, but be sure to avoid those which have been treated with fire-retardants or those in which cyanide is used in their manufacture as these types can be poisonous to fish.

Plastic mouldings These are becoming very popular because of their enormous surface area. They range from plastic shapes used in the biochemical industry, such as tubular pieces of UPVC, to household items, such as hair rollers, which are much cheaper and just as good.

Filter brushes An idea that has gained favour for both mechanical and biological filtration is to pass the water through a series of long-bristled brushes. The bristles sieve out a great deal of suspended solid material and provide a generous surface area on which nitrifying bacteria can thrive. Cleaning is simply a matter of opening the drain cock and gently shaking the rods that support the rows of filter brushes.

Zeolite This is a chemical filter medium which removes nitrates and ammonia from the water. It comes in the form of off-white or light-brown chippings of various sizes, and is made of hydrated silicates of calcium and aluminium, sometimes with sodium and potassium. Keep it in a container that can be easily removed for recharging. Do this by soaking the chippings overnight in a concentrated salt solution. After rinsing and drying, they are ready for further use in the filter system.

Below: *Various filter media.*
1 Filter brush, effective as both a mechanical and biological filter.
2 Commercially produced plastic mouldings. 3 Canterbury Spar gravel. 4 Large grade zeolite.
5 Baked clay granules. 6 Small grade zeolite chippings. 7 The effect of malachite green on zeolite.
8 Processed lava. 9 Freeze-dried bacteria to 'seed' biological filters.

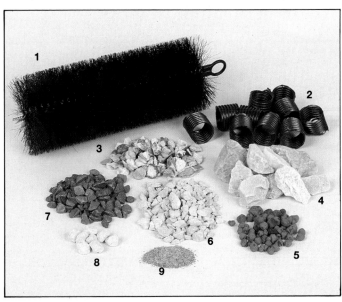

Filter designs

There is a wide range of filters on the market. These cater for everyone, from the beginner with a small pond to the specialist with a large pool full of many valuable fishes.

Multipurpose filters Basic designs consist of a large plastic container equipped with standard plumbing fittings. The water is pumped up to them from the pond and it then flows up or down, depending on the design, through a filter medium held in one main chamber. This type of filter is quite unsightly and so needs to be disguised in some way. You can let it into the ground provided that the outflow pipe is above the pond water level, or you can keep it above ground and disguise it as a wellhead by constructing a stone wall around it. Pre-filters are available that fit on to the inflow of the pump. These trap larger particles of debris before they reach the main filter, thereby prolonging its life and overcoming the need for frequent back-flushing.

Above: *A single-chamber filter with six rows of filter brushes, plus zeolite granules in the exit port.*

Upflow filter

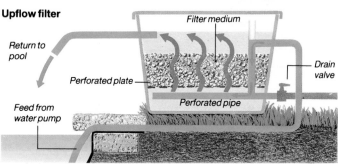

Filter medium

Return to pool

Perforated plate

Drain valve

Perforated pipe

Feed from water pump

Above: *A stylized upflow filter in action. A variety of filter media can be used in the single chamber, typically Canterbury Spar gravel.*

Below: *In the summer, when the water is warm and the fish active, position the pump further from the filter to create currents in the water.*

Summer set-up

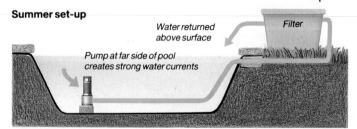

Water returned above surface

Filter

Pump at far side of pool creates strong water currents

Left: *A submersible pump that could be used to supply the filter systems shown on these pages.*

Above: *A basic filter chamber fitted with filter brushes being used to maintain Koi at an exhibition.*

Downflow filter

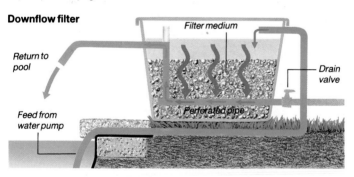

Filter medium

Return to pool

Drain valve

Feed from water pump

Perforated pipe

Above: *The working principles of a simple downflow filter. A perforated pipe buried in the filter medium carries water back to the pond.*

Below: *In the winter, position the pump further off the bottom and closer to the filter, and return the water to the pond more 'smoothly'.*

Winter set-up

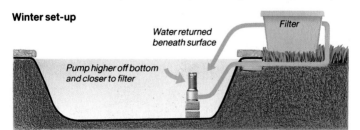

Water returned beneath surface

Filter

Pump higher off bottom and closer to filter

Larger filtration systems for the specialist with very big pools consist of several chambers. The first one will be a settlement chamber where large debris falls to the bottom and may be siphoned out or removed by a drain cock. The subsequent chambers operate on an over-and-under system, each one containing a different medium to carry out a specialized cleaning function. The second chamber will contain a coarse filtering medium, such as filter brushes, then the next chamber could contain Canterbury Spar and the final one, zeolite – as shown on this page.

In most cases, these multi-chamber filters are gravity fed by a large-bore pipe (10-25cm/4-10in in diameter) and the water is returned to the pond by a pump in the final filter chamber. This method is used to reduce the velocity into the filter to a minimum and thus allow maximum settlement of suspended solids from the inflowing water.

These types of filters hold very large volumes of water, but this is necessary in relation to the total volume of the pond. Commercial models can be very expensive, although it is quite possible to make your own from basic components.

Right: *Installing a multichamber filter system. The large bore gravity feed pipe to the first chamber can be seen at bottom right. The discharge box is at the extreme left.*

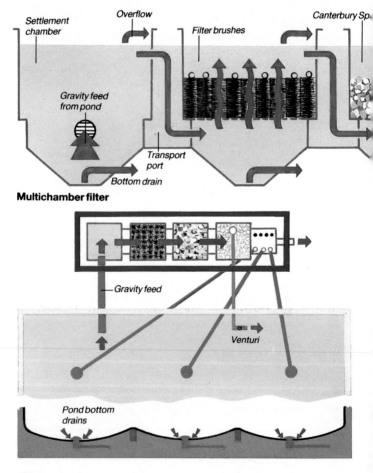

Settlement chamber

Overflow

Filter brushes

Canterbury Sp

Gravity feed from pond

Transport port

Bottom drain

Multichamber filter

Gravity feed

Venturi

Pond bottom drains

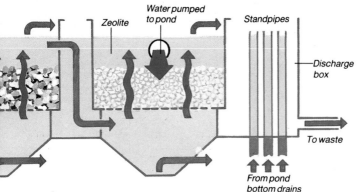

Left: *A plan view showing how the above filter could relate to a large pond. Each of the three areas of the pond can be drained individually.* Below: *A side view showing the gravity feed pipe from the pond to the settlement chamber of the filter.*

Above: *A typical multichamber filter system in action. Each chamber has a separate bottom drain for cleaning purposes, and a system of valves allows pond water to bypass certain chambers – when treating the water with disease remedies, for example.*

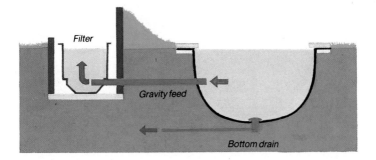

87

Undergravel filter This type of biological filter is essentially a larger version of the system used in aquariums. The aim is identical in both cases: to set up a constant water flow through a bed of gravel at the bottom of the aquarium/pond in which aerobic nitrifying bacteria can flourish to purify the water as it passes through. Since the design and size of ponds varies so widely, you will need to construct the necessary pipework from basic components. Use PVC pipes of 37mm (1.5in) bore and build up a suitable framework using 'T' pieces, elbows and cross-pieces to cover at least one third of the pond's floor area. Drill 6mm (0.25in) diameter holes at intervals along spacing these about 20cm (8in) apart on the tubes near the outflow pump connection and lessening the distance between them down to about 10cm (4in) in the 'outlying' areas of the grid. This will help to set up an even water flow over the entire area of the filter. Drill the holes in pairs at an angle of 45° from the bottom of the grid, as shown in the illustration.

Place a plastic mesh with 12mm (0.5in) perforations over the framework of pipes – this will prevent clogging – and build up a brick enclosure around the edges. Add a layer of gravel (1cm/0.4in particle size) to a depth of 20-30cm (8-12in) over the grid and connect the system to a submerged or external water pump. When turned on, the pump will draw water downwards through the gravel, into the pipes and then back to the pond through the outlet side of the pump.

Left to itself, and with the pump running, the gravel bed will develop a thriving colony of aerobic bacteria over a period of several weeks. This maturation period depends on the temperature of the water and on the presence of suitable organic wastes to 'seed' the process. To speed matters up, it is possible to add sachets of freeze-dried bacteria that in ideal conditions will 'mature' the gravel bed in seven to ten days.

Since the bacteria need a constant flow of oxygen-rich water to thrive, it is essential to keep the pump running continuously. If it is switched off for any length of time, the colonies of aerobic bacteria in the gravel will die, often with dire results for the fish since the dead bacteria release toxins.

Undergravel filter

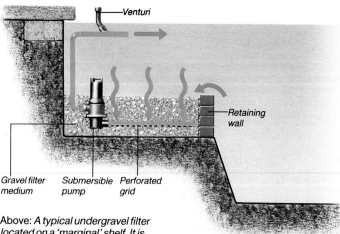

Above: *A typical undergravel filter located on a 'marginal' shelf. It is important to keep the water flowing through the gravel bed to maintain the aerobic bacteria that perform the biological cleaning action.*

Right: *A cutaway of the filter shows how the gridwork of pipes draws in water from the entire gravel bed.*

Vegetable filter

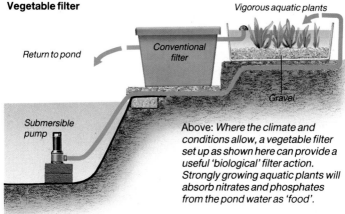

Above: Where the climate and conditions allow, a vegetable filter set up as shown here can provide a useful 'biological' filter action. Strongly growing aquatic plants will absorb nitrates and phosphates from the pond water as 'food'.

Vegetable filter This is basically another type of biological filter, but filled with growing plants rather than a bacteria-rich medium; Japanese and Chinese fish-breeders, in particular, use this system. For any pond, it simply involves setting up a second pond or container at a higher level planted with vigorous aquatic plants, such as *Sagittaria* sp. (Arrowhead), *Eichhornia crassipes* (Water Hyacinth) and, only in warm climates, *Pistia stratiotes* (Water Lettuce). These aquatic plants are greedy feeders and will absorb nitrates and phosphates from the pond water pumped into the container. An overflow pipe from this 'vegetable filter' can direct the water to a more conventional filter system on its way back to the main pond. The only maintenance required is to thin out the plants periodically, thereby removing the salts at the same time (i.e. incorporated in plant tissue). Naturally, this type of filtration system will work more effectively, and over a longer period, in warmer rather than cold climates.

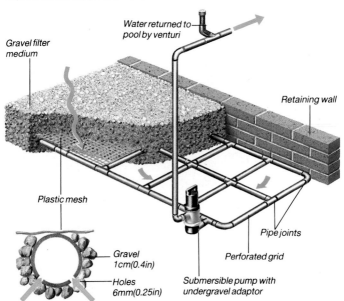

Sand pressure filters These are more popularly associated with swimming pools, but they are also used in Koi ponds. However, they are usually used as a supplement to biological filters, the sand acting as an efficient mechanical filter to any suspended solids still in the water. Because they can be back-flushed easily, they do not clog up as often as other models which use diaformaceous earth as the filter medium. Various sizes are available.

General filter requirements
Whether you are buying a filter or creating your own system, there are certain factors to be taken into consideration, particularly for filters with a biological action, which will take some months to reach optimum efficiency; guard against initial overstocking.

Surface area The surface area of the filter medium determines the number of bacteria that can colonize the system. This in turn dictates the rate at which ammonia and other toxic wastes are removed and, consequently, the health and growthrate of the fishes.

Volume of filter material The volume of filter material should not be less than 10-15 percent of the volume of the pond and, in any event, should not be less than $0.5m^3$ ($17.6ft^3$).

In the case of plastic filter media, the weight of fish that $1m^3$ ($35.3ft^3$) of filter medium is capable of supporting depends on the amount of ammonia produced in the pond. Normally $1m^3$ will support 75kg (185lb) of fish. This assumes that the recommended feeding schedule is followed, that the fish are a uniform size of 30-45cm (12-18in), and that the filter is sufficiently mature and well aerated.

Flowrate The flow of water through the filter must be 'in tune' with the filtration processes at work. If it is too powerful, for example, it will prevent the build up of a beneficial colony of bnacteria by tending to dislodge them.

Below: *A sand pressure filter. These units are available in various sizes. A 'multiport' valve controls water inflow and outflow, back-flushing and rinsing.*

Sand pressure filter

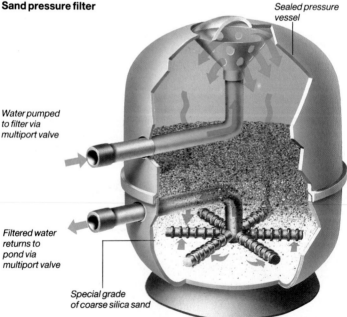

Sealed pressure vessel

Water pumped to filter via multiport valve

Filtered water returns to pond via multiport valve

Special grade of coarse silica sand

Oxygen concentration The water flowing over the filter medium must be well oxygenated. Tests carried out on the outflow from the filter should still reveal an appreciable level of oxygen in the water.

Aeration systems
Many systems are used to increase the oxygen concentration in the water. Most of them involve quite bulky structures, such as air-exposure towers, which are located outside the pond. However, a small submersible device successfully used in commercial fish farms is now available for domestic ponds. This is known as a mat aerator and it gives excellent results. Basically, it consists of a plastic or stainless steel cylinder which, for pond use, is available in diameters of 5-10cm (2-4in). Air is supplied to the unit by a blower operating at a pressure just sufficient to overcome the static head (pressure exerted by the water above it) and friction losses. The air is first delivered to a diffuser in the base of the unit. As it rises, the air acts as an air-lift pump, moving the mixture of diffused air and water upwards through the cylinder.

Principle of the venturi
Below: *The principle of the venturi tube, named after the Italian physicist who devised it. A restriction in the pipe causes the water flow to accelerate and the resulting drop in pressure brings in air to create a turbulent air/water mixture. A simple way of regulating the amount of air is shown at right.*

Venturi rings (normally three) deflect the air and water mixture on to three free-turning turbines, the centre turbine rotating counter to the others. The combined effect is to shear the air bubbles into a froth of tiny bubbles, causing turbulence in the mixture and impeding the upward flow. The air/water interface is thus maximized, giving an extremely high oxygen saturation level. In addition, substantial aeration occurs in the surface boil caused by rising air bubbles.

Less complicated aeration devices can also be used. An aquarium air pump in a waterproof housing will supply a small amount of air, for example, and will work best fitted with a lime-wood airstone. The venturi is a popular system which can be made or bought. To make one, place a small restriction in the return pipe from the filter so that the passage is narrowed but not blocked. Bore a hole in the pipe just after the restriction and cement an airline pipe into position. As the water pushes past the restriction, it will create a partial vacuum which will draw air into the tube.

Cap on air intake tube

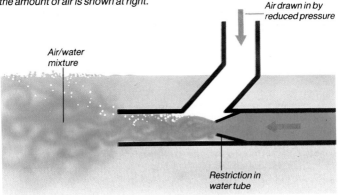

Air/water mixture

Air drawn in by reduced pressure

Restriction in water tube

Pond maintenance

One is often asked about the amount of upkeep or maintenance a pond requires, but the answer depends on a number of factors that vary from pond to pond. One pond may need very little care, whereas another, due to its size, the plants and fishes that it has been stocked with, and the type of water and construction used, will need a steady flow of attention throughout the year.

Let us take as an example a pond that has a complicated shape with narrow inlets, shallow shelving water and overhanging trees. The shape will at once encourage parts of the water to stagnate; the shallows will breed algae; and leaves will drop from the trees into the water, causing putrefaction. The insect population will increase in certain groups, weeds will run riot, and diseases affecting plants and fishes will increase too.

If we take an alternative pond, with a simple shape so that the water can circulate freely, placed in the open, with a balance of plants and livestock, then the amount of attention it needs will be minimal – only an occasional thinning of plants if they become too rampant, and checking the fishes for health and vigour.

Leaves

If you live in a wooded area, autumn leaves can be a problem, falling into the water and sinking to the bottom where they decompose and give off noxious gases. To prevent this occurring, spread a fine net over the water surface to catch the leaves; where there is a large stretch of water, lay the net in sections across the pond so that they can be lifted off piecemeal to remove the leaves.

Weather problems

Weather, too, can cause some additional upkeep. Frost may seal off the water surface, preventing oxygen from reaching the unfrozen water and stopping toxic gases escaping; this is not critical over a short period, as the cold will have made the fishes slow down and they need less oxygen, but there is a danger of ice expanding and cracking or splitting the pond container, whether it is a precast shell, a liner or a concrete pond.

If the pond has been designed with sloping sides the ice will be forced upwards without damaging the structure. A pond heater can be floated in the pond; when switched on, this will keep a small area unfrozen around it, allowing both oxygen and fishes to reach the surface, and when the ice expands the pond container will not be damaged. A cheaper method is to drop a large floating ball into the water, and remove it when the water freezes, to leave a hole in the ice for air

Tall canes will obstruct a heron's flight path and deter it from robbing the pool of pet fish.

Nets are important to lift fish for health examination, as is the spiky tool for removing pondweed.

To prevent ice from sealing the water surface, a pond heater is highly recommended.

to reach the unfrozen water; replace it at night when the temperature drops. The expanding ice will lift the ball, and thus also lower the risk of pond damage by relieving pressure.

Never break the ice with a heavy blow, because the shock waves will pass through the water and can stun or kill the fishes. It is better to use a hot object, a metal bar or a can filled with boiling water, to melt the ice, which can then be lifted off and broken up away from the pond. Sometimes if the weather continues freezing it pays to drain off some water under the ice, leaving 2.5cm (1in) or so of air between ice and water; this will act as a form of insulation, and still keep some oxygen in touch with the water.

In very hot weather there is a danger that a small pond will get too warm and the oxygen level become dangerously low, causing the death of the fishes. To prevent this, increase the level of oxygen by pumping the water through a fountain; the drops of water will be recharged with oxygen before returning to the pond.

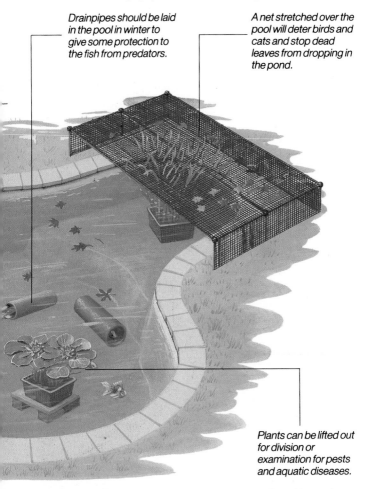

Drainpipes should be laid in the pool in winter to give some protection to the fish from predators.

A net stretched over the pool will deter birds and cats and stop dead leaves from dropping in the pond.

At the end of the season the pump has to be lifted out and serviced and thoroughly cleaned.

Plants can be lifted out for division or examination for pests and aquatic diseases.

The health and safety of the pool can be kept at a high level by a little care and regular maintenance to prevent trouble before it starts.

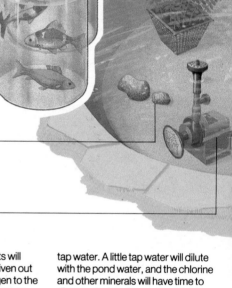

Plants can be gently lowered into the pond, resting on bricks for the soil to absorb water.

Extra oxygenating plants are helpful in hot weather to increase the oxygen level in the water.

When removing fish from the pool while repair or cleaning is undertaken, keep them in a wide-necked vessel so that the maximum amount of air can reach the surface.

If the water is acid, a piece of limestone or chalk can be put in it to balance it.

In hot weather when the oxygen level is low, keep the pump running to aerate the water.

Additional oxygenating plants will absorb the carbon dioxide given out by the fishes and return oxygen to the water, and help the pond balance; they will also prevent sunlight from reaching some areas of water and thus stop the growth and spread of algae, which increase in hot weather.

Another thing to watch for in hot weather is the rapid evaporation of water. This can lower the surface quite dramatically and expose the liner, if one has been used; sunlight on exposed plastic can speed up deterioration, making the liner brittle and hard so that it cracks, allowing the water to seep away.

When the pond level drops, top it up using a hose. Because the water needs time to adjust to the surrounding temperature, it is better to top up with a little extra water several times, rather than to allow the surface to drop a long way and then have to pour in large quantities of raw

tap water. A little tap water will dilute with the pond water, and the chlorine and other minerals will have time to disperse before the next topping up takes place; this will cause less distress to the livestock.

Occasionally the pond will have a sudden influx of algae, usually after aquatic plants have been thinned out and fed, especially if this coincides with a period of uninterrupted sunshine. This sometimes happens when you wish to show off the pond to friends, and an immediate remedy is called for. The answer is to use a dose of algaecide, which can be obtained from most aquatic centres and specialist shops.

If the water becomes too acid, due to rain or seepage, it is important to redress the balance. This can be done by placing a lump of limestone or chalk in the water until it becomes neutral again. Use a water testing kit to check the pH value finally.

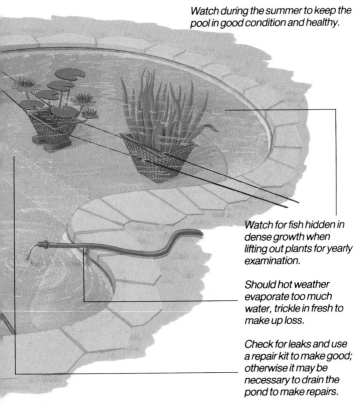

Watch during the summer to keep the pool in good condition and healthy.

Watch for fish hidden in dense growth when lifting out plants for yearly examination.

Should hot weather evaporate too much water, trickle in fresh to make up loss.

Check for leaks and use a repair kit to make good; otherwise it may be necessary to drain the pond to make repairs.

Structural repairs

Leaks can occur with most ponds, but are more likely to happen if you use cheaper materials than with the more expensive and robust ones. The commonest problem is the accidental piercing of the liner with a sharp point, which permits the water to seep away. Kits are supplied by the manufacturers for repairing this type of damage, and the manufacturer's instructions should be followed to ensure a good and lasting repair. This also goes for the precast pool shells.

With concrete the process is more difficult, and often entails draining, cleaning and painting the entire pond area with a repair medium, which can be either a liquid plastic or a bitumen-based paint. An alternative that has become quite popular is to line the concrete pond with a liner.

On the rare occasions when the pond has to be drained – either for repair or to remove debris, overgrown plants or too many fishes – a temporary pond should be set up. This can be made by using a piece of liner material laid inside a large box; or use a series of large bottles with wide mouths or large plastic containers, if they have a large water surface open to the air. The fishes should be caught with a net and transferred into a smooth plastic bowl before taking them out of the pond; this will prevent damage to their scales and the subsequent danger of disease.

Plants can be lifted out, but check that there are no fishes secreted in the matt of stems and leaves. Remove the remaining livestock by hand. Clean or repair the pond and refill it with water. Allow the chlorine to disperse before replacing the plants, and then gradually put back the cheapest fishes first to test the water; if they are fine, then add your prize specimens and keep a careful eye on the pond for the next few days.

PART 3

PLANTS FOR THE POND

A pond would not be complete without plants, and even those ponds containing vegetarian-minded fishes can still have attractive plants associated with them, albeit at the pondside.

Such is the diversity of suitable and attractive plants for the pond environment that it can be hard to know exactly where to begin, or where to draw the line. Many species are very happy either completely or partly in the water. Thanks to marshy species, the pond can be integrated quite easily into the garden, with water and land merging imperceptibly, just as nature intended. Although pondside and in-pond plants may both be chosen for their beauty and decorative qualities, the truly aquatic species have other very important functions on which the pond depends, almost for its very life.

One obvious difference between terrestrial and aquatic species is that land plants can, literally, stand up for themselves; aquatic plants have no need for stiff stems as they are supported by the surrounding water. Additionally, water-dwelling plants do not necessarily take in nutrients only through their roots; many absorb nourishment directly through the leaves, and here is the real value of water plants. By this action, they help to keep the water conditions pure – they absorb carbon dioxide and give off excess oxygen during the hours of daylight; they actively starve out algae, which would otherwise cloud the water; they also reduce the level of nitrates in the water. Their floating leaves bring welcome shade and shelter to the fish, and newly hatched fish (or small amphibians) can shelter between their stems, safe from predators; some may even have begun life there – as quietly hatching fish eggs or, like the newt in its egg, wrapped up in a single leaf.

Right: *A wealth of colourful plants can be grown in and around the pond, as shown here.*

Oxygenating plants

Oxygenating plants provide shelter for spawning fish and their fry, as well as releasing oxygen directly into the water in strong light. They also take up mineral salts from the water that would normally encourage the growth of algae. A dozen or so should be planted in a small container and allow one container to every 2m² (22ft²) in a small pool, but as the pool enlarges relatively fewer containers are needed; a pool of over 55m² (586ft²) would require twenty containers. If the plants become too prolific it is a simple matter to lift out a few containers to allow more space. The following is a selection of useful oxygenating plants.

Elodea (Anacharis) canadensis (1)
Canadian Pond Weed; Water Thyme
This plant originates in North America and has dark green, small thyme-like leaves with fine serrations. It

increases mainly by the slender and brittle stems rooting at each whorl of leaves. Provided it is pruned of all dead growth it should never die. Keep it in a container to prevent it spreading unduly. *E. callitrichoides* is a finer and more delicate variety.

Fontinalis antipyretica (2)
Willow Moss
Forms dark green clumps and prefers to root in gravel, pebbles and stonework; it is best seen in moving water. The new shoots send out light green buds on the ends of the stems, which are mossy in appearance and harbour many varieties of animal life.

Hottonia palustris (3)
Water Violet; Featherfoil
The plant has feathery bright green leaves under water; only the flower stem rises above the surface and bears pale lilac blooms. It should be

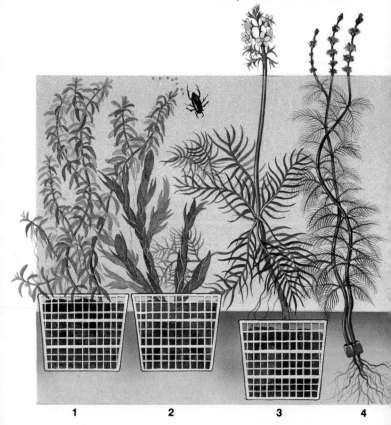

1   2   3   4

planted separately with a piece of the creeping root attached. In autumn the plant forms winter buds that sink into the pool floor to reappear in the spring. The American form *H. inflata* has white flowers.

Lagarosiphon major (Elodea crispa)

A very good oxygenator with curly leaves on long trailing stems.

Myriophyllum (4)
Milfoil

The delicate feathery leaves are characteristic of this group of plants; most will grow under water and give good service as oxygenators. They are very decorative. A portion of the plant can be weighted and sunk into the pool, where it will quickly root and grow. *M. alterniflorum, spicatum*, and *verticillatum* are all good species to grow and are widely available.

Potamogeton crispus (6)
Curly Pondweed

This plant has long wiry stems with wavy-edged leaves of a shiny brown that give it the appearance of seaweed. It enhances the look of most ponds and is ideal in moving water; plant in clumps near the pump or at the base of a waterfall.

Rorippa nasturtium aquaticum (5)
Water Cress

This plant grows wild in the Northern Hemisphere and is well known for its culinary uses. Plant cuttings directly into containers of fine soil in shallow water and trim it regularly to keep it looking neat. A good oxygenator.

Tillaea recurva (7)

An Australian plant of creeping habit that grows well either submerged or at the water margin. It has very fine stems and leaves with tiny flowers.

5   6   7

Deep water and marginal plants

There are many aquatic plants that grow in deep water. Their roots need soil and this is best kept in a container, allowing the plant to be lifted out of the water for pruning, treating for pests and diseases and for feeding. The container can be a box, pot, basket or a proprietary plastic container. The soil should be plain with the addition of bonemeal; some charcoal lumps will help to keep the soil sweet.

Some plants float on the surface with trailing roots that pick up nutrients from the water and these can be easily lifted out and thinned if they spread too far.

Marginal plants in the main have their rootstocks just under the water with their leaves and flowers held well above the surface. Here again, containers should be used to allow the plant to be lifted out, thinned and stopped from taking over the pond. Many aquatic plants are invasive.

Acorus (1, 2)
Sweet Flag
A group of plants of which *A. calamus* (1), which comes from wide areas in the Northern Hemisphere, and *A. gramineus* (2) from Japan are the two most popular. *A. calamus* has sword-shaped leaves like an iris and flowers that are densely packed on short spurs more like an arum. It reaches a height of about 60-75cm (24-30in). *A. gramineus* is finer with narrow leaves and reaches only 20-30cm (8-12in) tall. A variegated variety is available.

Alisma (3)
Water Plantain
Two varieties are grown as aquatics, *A. lanceolatum* and *A. plantago-aquatica*. These similar plants both originate in the Northern Hemisphere and grow to 15-30cm (6-12in) tall. Spikes of small pink flowers rise above the oval leaves. This plant is quick to establish in the pond.

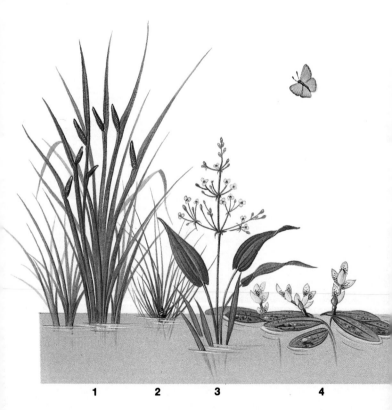

1   2   3   4

Aponogeton distachyus (4)
Water Hawthorn
This South African plant is very decorative, with oblong floating leaves and spikes of scented flowers that rise above the water surface. *A distachyus* is the hardiest of the family and flowers from early spring to late autumn. This adaptable plant can be grown from tubers or from seed and will thrive in very shallow water or as deep as 45cm (18in).

Azolla (6)
Fairy Moss
Azolla caroliniana and *A. filiculoides* are two very similar plants native to South America. They are floating plants that form mats of fine fronds on the surface, with the roots taking nourishment from the water. The leaves turn from a fresh green in summer to reddish autumnal tints. In severe climates they are best over-wintered in a pan and kept frost-free.

Butomus umbellatus (5)
Flowering Rush
Native to Europe and Asia, this plant is equally at home in marshland, shallow or deep water. It has long thin green leaves, triangular in section, and bears up to 30 pink or purple flowers in each flowerhead that arise like inverted umbrellas from early summer to early autumn. The plant can reach 1.2m (4ft) tall.

Calla palustris (7)
Bog Arum
Found in the wild in North America, Northern Europe and Asia, this plant has dark green heart-shaped leaves and a creeping rootstock that grows happily in and out of the water. It can be propagated by dividing the roots into sections. The white flowers resemble those of the Arum Lily. After pollination by pond snails, the female flowers mature to red berries. It grows to about 15-20cm (6-8in) in height.

5   **6**   **7**

Caltha (1)
Kingcup; Marsh Marigold
Native to North America and Europe, these plants have round serrated leaves and buttercup-like flowers of a golden yellow. The single forms can be grown from seed or root division. Varieties to look for are *C. alba* (white), *C. palustris*, *C. polypetala* and the double form *C. palustris plena*. They grow in shallow water or wet mud and vary in height from 20cm (8in) to 90cm (3ft), depending on variety.

Carex (2)
Sedge
These perennials from Europe are grass-like and most are very invasive; they should be contained to prevent their spreading. *C. riparia* 'Bowles' Golden', with golden leaves and brown flowers, is recommended as being the least invasive of the genus. It grows to over 30cm (12in) tall.

Cyperus (3)
Umbrella Grass
From Chile and Europe, these sedge-like plants bear clumps of green or brown flowers arranged on stems like an umbrella. *C. eragrostis* is normally hardy and about 60cm (2ft) tall while *C. longus* is hardier but very invasive; reaching up to 1.2m (4ft) in height. The dark green stems of *C. longus* provide excellent cut material for use in flower arrangements. They should not be grown in deep water.

Echinodorus (4)
These plants from North America and Europe have oval leaves on long stems and bur-like heads; these should be removed to prevent seeding. Flowers are white or pinkish white. *E. ranunculoides* grows up to 45cm (18in), *E. radicans* (not hardy in severe climates) to 1.2m (4ft), and *E. rostratus* (Burhead) to 30cm (12in).

1   2   3   4

Eichhornia crassipes (5)
Water Hyacinth

A prolific species from the tropics, this plant is suited to areas subject to frost as this kills the plant before it can become too invasive. Roots should be lifted and kept just moist from early autumn to late spring and then floated again in the pond during the summer. The leaves are heart shaped and the lilac flowers, borne on spikes up to 38cm (15in) high, are spectacular. The plant spreads to 45cm (18in) wide in one season.

Eriophorum (6)
Bog Cotton; Cotton Grass

A wild plant in the Northern Hemisphere, this genus has grass-like leaves and cotton-like seedheads. *E. angustifolium* grows to 30cm (12in) tall, *E. latifolium* to 45cm (18in) and *E. vaginatum* barely reaches 30cm (12in). All thrive in shallow water or wet mud and can be grown from seed or by root division.

Glyceria aquatica variegata (7)
Manna Grass

A European plant with grass-like leaves arranged in clumps and striped in white, yellow and green with a pink hue in spring and autumn. It will reach 90cm (3ft) if unrestricted but will be only a third of this height if it is grown in a smallish container. Propagate from side shoots.

Houttuynia cordata (8)
From the mountainous regions of the Himalayas through to Japan, this attractive plant has heart-shaped, blue-green leaves, red stems and white flowers with a large central cone. It grows in shallow water and will reach 45-50cm (18-20in) tall. Increase by root division. A double form, *H.c. plena*, is available.

5   6   7   8

Hydrocharis morsus-ranae (1)
Frogbit

A floating plant from Europe with bright green, fleshy, kidney-shaped leaves and small white flowers with three petals. Snails and water beetles enjoy the foliage. Terminal buds drop to the bottom of the pond in the autumn and sprout in the following spring; the rest of the plant decays.

Hypericum elodes (2)
Marsh Hypericum

A European plant up to 30cm (12in) tall that makes a good marginal specimen. It has dense rounded foliage and creeping stems covered with fine downy hair. The flowers are yellow and appear in late summer. Increase by dividing the roots.

Iris (3)
Iris; Yellow Flag

A large family of plants with members from many parts of the world: a few thrive in wet conditions. *I. kaempferi* enjoys summer wetness but needs to be dry during the winter; it is best grown in a container that can be removed from the water on to dry land in the autumn and replaced in the spring. The flowers appear in midsummer on stems up to 90cm (3ft) tall. Many varieties are available with single or double blooms in shades of blue, lavender, purple, pink and white. The 'Higo' strain is particularly beautiful. *I. laevigata* enjoys water all the year, producing blue or white flowers. *I. pseudacorus* revels in water up to 45cm (18in) deep, bearing superb yellow flowers on stems up to 1.5m (5ft) high in early summer. *I.p.* 'Variegata' has yellow flowers and yellow-striped foliage. *I. versicolor,* an American plant, produces violet-blue blooms in early summer on 60cm (24in) stems. The lovely variety 'Kermesina' has wine-red flowers in early summer. All these irises can be increased by dividing the rhizome after flowering.

1   2   3   4

Juncus (4)
Rush

A large family spread throughout the world, but only a few species are recommended for the garden pond as they are invasive; all have grass-like leaves. *J. bufonis* has reddish flowers and grows to 20cm (8in) tall. *J. effusus* var. *spiralis* (4) has curious spiral green stems reaching 45cm (18in) in height and *J. ensifolius* has dark brown to blackish flowerheads held 30cm (12in) high. All enjoy either shallow water or moist soil. Be sure to avoid the invasive species.

Mentha aquatica (5)
Water Mint

A European plant with both bright green and brown aromatic leaves, that grows well in either moist soil or shallow water. The lavender blue flowers are borne in clusters. It normally grows to 30cm (12in) tall, but in rich soil it can reach 1m (3.3ft). Increase by division of roots.

Menyanthus trifoliata (6)
Bog Bean; Buck Bean

A Northern Hemisphere plant with light green trifoliate leaves and spikes of rosy white flowers in early summer. It spreads by means of a horizontal rootstock, which makes it suitable for covering pond edges; it grows only about 30cm (12in) tall. Keep this plant constricted and cut it back if it is too vigorous for its chosen site.

Mimulus (7)
Monkey Flower; Monkey Musk

A group of annuals and perennials, mostly from North America; they flower in late summer with red, yellow and orange blooms. *M. guttatus* grows to 45cm (18in) tall with single yellow flowers blotched with crimson. The 'hose-in-hose' varieties have semi-double flowers. *M. cupreus*, *M. lewisii*, *M. maculosus*, *M. moschatus*, *M. ringens* and *M. tigrinus* are all worth growing. They vary in height from 20cm (8in) to 90cm (3ft).

5   6   7

Miscanthus sacchariflorus
Hardy Sugar Cane
This American plant, up to 1.8m (6ft) tall, has the appearance of an ornamental grass and bears flowers noted for the groups of silky hairs at their bases. *M.s. variegata* has white and green variegated foliage.

Myosotis palustris (3)
Water Forget-Me-Not
A plant from Europe with many historical and legendary associations. It is ideal for the pool edge, reaching 20cm (8in) tall and bearing bright blue flowers. It seeds well and thrives even in the shade. An improved version, 'Mermaid', has larger and brighter blue flowers. An excellent choice.

Nuphar (1)
Yellow Water Lily; Spatterdock
These water lily-like plants from North America, Europe and Japan have both submerged and floating leaves; the submerged ones are finely divided, the floating ones oval and leathery. The plants have a creeping rootstock and bear yellow flowers from late spring to early autumn. All grow well in deep and shady water. Some varieties are very vigorous and should be controlled by using containers. For small ponds choose the free-flowering *Nuphar minima*.

Nymphoides peltata (Villarsia nymphoides; Limnanthemum peltatum) (2)
Floating Heart; Water Fringe
A lily-like aquatic plant with rounded floating bright green leaves with crinkled edges. The flowers are yellow, blooming in later summer and held just above the water surface. It will grow well in either deep or shallow water and should be kept in a container to curb its invasive nature.

Orontium aquaticum (4)
Golden Club
A North American plant with strap-shaped floating leaves in deep water; in shallow water the leaves stand up to 45cm (18in) above the surface. They are dark blue-green on the

1   2   3   4

upper surface and silver on the undersides. The flowers appear in spring and early summer, yellow in colour and borne on conspicuous white stems. Grow from seed in shallow water and then transplant to deeper water or to soil.

Peltandra
Arrow Arum

There are two North American species, *P. alba* and *P. virginica*. The former has arrow-shaped leaves and white arum-like flowers followed by red berries; the latter has green flowers and green berries. Both grow up to 75cm (30in) in height and can be increased by dividing the rootstock.

Pontederia cordata (5)
Pickerel Weed

A marshland plant from North America, *P. cordata* has shiny heart-shaped deep green leaves and bears blue flowers in late summer. The plant will make large clumps, but they are easily split for smaller areas. It grows up to a height of about 60cm (2ft). A

less hardy species, *P. lanceolata*, has longer lance-like leaves and can reach 1.5m (5ft) in height.

Ranunculus lingua grandiflora (6)
Spearwort

An improved form of a European plant, with narrow leaves and large yellow flowers similar to those of the buttercup; these appear in late spring and summer. It grows to a height of 90cm (3ft) and can be increased by dividing the rootstock. The stems are thick and deep pink in colour. Contain the roots to stop the plant spreading too far and taking over the pond.

Sagittaria (7)
Arrowhead

These plants from Europe and Asia are not generally recommended for a small pond; *S. sagittifolia* and *S. japonica flore pleno* are the two that are suitable; the former needs a container to prevent it spreading. They have distinctive arrow-shaped leaves and white flowers in midsummer. Up to 45cm (18in).

5   6   7

Saururus (1)
Lizard's Tail

From North America comes *Saururus cernuus* and from China and Japan, *S. chinensis*. These plants have dark green heart-shaped leaves and sprays of scented flowers in summer; the former white, the latter cream. Both can reach 45cm (18in) tall.

Scirpus (2)
Apart from two varieties, these plants should not be used as they are too invasive. Even these two should have their roots contained to prevent them from being too vigorous in growth. *S. albescens* has white variegations on the narrow green leaves; it will reach 1.2m (4ft) tall. *S. tabernaemontanii* var. *zebrinus* (Porcupine Quill Rush; Zebra Rush) has green and white bands on the stems and grows to 90cm (3ft) high. Increase both by root division in the spring.

Stratiotes aloides (3)
Water Soldier

A floating plant, found wild in Europe, with sword-like leaves radiating from a central crown. The flowers are small and white; after flowering the plants sink under the surface and produce side shoots that lie dormant until the following spring. Water Soldiers grow to 30cm (1ft) across and prefer alkaline water.

Thalia dealbata (4)
Water Canna

A North American plant with spear-shaped leaves and long spikes of deep purple flowers. In mild areas it can be left to overwinter in the pond, but it requires protection from frost. If in doubt, lift the plants and keep them under cover until late spring. It can grow to 1.8m (6ft) tall in good conditions and can be increased by dividing the rootstock.

1   2   3   4

Trapa natans (5)
Water Chestnut
This annual floating plant from southern Europe has triangular serrated leaves of a bright glossy green. The flowers are small and white and the black seeds (nuts) are large with four spines, and edible. They can be left to ripen on the plant and germinated the following spring.

Typha (6)
Reedmace
These European plants are commonly and erroneously called bulrushes because they have tall grass-like leaves and distinctive brown heads of flowers. They are very invasive and only two are suitable for the garden pond: *T. angustifolia*, which reaches 1.2m (4ft) high, and *T. minima*, which is smaller in scale and only grows to 45cm (18in) tall. Increase both by root division.

Villarsia nymphoides (7)
Floating Heart; Water Fringe
This plant is described under its alternative name of *Nymphoides peltata* on page 60.

Zantedeschia aethiopica (8)
Arum Lily; Lily of the Nile
From Africa, this plant has glossy green leaves and spectacular white flowers during the summer months. It grows up to 90cm (3ft) in height. The true flowers are tiny and yellow, and massed on a central column, or spadix, which is partially enclosed by a showy white modified leaf called a spathe. The plant needs some protection from winter frosts, although hardy varieties are being introduced. One of these is 'Crowborough'. Provide plenty of water during the growing season in spring and summer and increase by dividing the rootstock.

5   6   7   8

Water lilies

The water lily is justifiably the most popular of water plants. It has brilliant blooms and at the same time its leaves cover the water surface to provide both shelter to fishes and welcome shade that prevents excessive algae growth. In addition, water lilies – all species and hybrids of *Nymphaea* – are available in a variety of sizes to suit the size and depth of any pond, from the pygmy types that need just a shallow covering of water to the more vigorous types that would swamp a small pond completely and need deep water to prevent the leaves from standing proud of the surface.

Water lilies should be grown in containers. They will give sufficient anchorage and nutrition while stopping the plant from outgrowing the pond. They will also allow easy access to the plant for maintenance, treatment for disease or pest attack, and feeding. Containers allow a certain flexibility of position and can be adjusted to give the right depth of water over the crown of the plant; this is achieved by inserting bricks or other inert material under the container to raise it.

There are two main groups of water lilies: the hardy and the tropical. In temperate zones the hardy ones are fine for outdoor ponds; the tropical lilies are only suited to indoor and outdoor ponds where the water temperature is maintained at 21°C (70°F) throughout the year.

The best soil to grow water lilies in

Pygmy water lilies

Pygmy varieties are suitable for small ponds with water to a depth of 23cm (9in). They spread to 1800cm^2 (2ft^2).

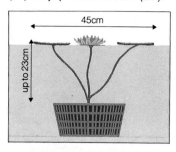

WHITE BLOOMS
candida small cup-shaped flowers with a red stigma.
odorata minor Small and scented blooms of pure white; the green leaves are red underneath.
'Pygmaea Alba' The smallest lily, with flowers barely 2.5cm (1in) across. It requires just 5cm (2in) of water over the crown and needs protection during hard frost.

Right: 'Laydekeri Lilacea', *with fine tiny rose-coloured scented blooms that deepen to red as they mature.*

Far right: 'Comanche' *has pink, orange and yellow blooms that are held well above the water surface.*

PINK AND ROSE BLOOMS
caroliniana Delicate perfumed medium-sized blooms of skin-pink.
'Laydekeri Lilacea' Rose-coloured scented cup-shaped blooms that deepen to red as they age. The leaves are dark green.
odorata 'W.B. Shaw' Very fragrant pink flowers with narrow petals carried above the water surface.

RED BLOOMS
'Ellisiana' Deep red flowers that darken to purple at the centre.
'Laydekeri purpurata' The blooms are bright rosy crimson with shading on the petals. Very free flowering.

is a heavy loam well fortified with bonemeal (approximately 0.1 litres per 4.5 litres of soil). Animal manures are not recommended as the water becomes over rich with nutrients that will encourage algae growth. Should the loam be poor quality and low in nitrogen mix some dried blood into the soil. The roots should be well anchored by ramming the soil well down in the container, leaving some room for a layer of shingle or gravel over the soil to prevent fish from stirring up the fine particles and making the water cloudy.

Water lilies need sun, plain soil and the right depth of water. Given these they will reward the gardener with a prolific show of flowers from early summer onwards.

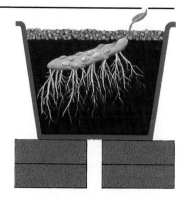

Above: *Water lilies should be planted in containers filled with a heavy loam with the growing tip just above the surface and a layer of stone chips to stop fish from stirring up the soil.*

'Maurice Laydekeri' Red flowers flecked with white.

pygmaea rubra Delicate rose blooms that age to dark red.

YELLOW AND ORANGE BLOOMS
'Aurora' The blooms start yellow and change to orange and then deepen to red. The leaves are mottled brown and green.

'Comanche' Deep apricot flowers turning to copper with orange centres. Young foliage is purple changing to green mottled with brown. The blooms are held well above the water surface.

'Graziella' Orange blooms. Very free flowering. Blooms 5-7.5cm (2-3in).

'Helvola' The smallest yellow water lily with pale yellow star-shaped flowers and golden centres. Young foliage is purple changing to green mottled with brown. The blooms are held well above the water surface.

'Indiana' Pink-orange blooms that turn to copper-red. Green leaves marked with purple.

odorata sulphureae Small spiky soft yellow flowers held above the water surface. Small spotted leaves.

'Paul Hariot' Yellow flowers that age through orange to red. Free flowering. Leaves marked in brown and green. Blooms 13-15cm (5-6in) across.

Small water lilies

These need 15-45cm (6-18in) of water depth and spread to 60cm (2ft) across when fully mature.

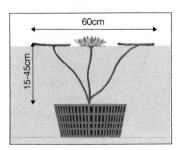

WHITE BLOOMS

'Albatross' Large white flowers with golden centres and erect petals. Young leaves are purple and turn to apple green as they mature.

caroliniana nivea Large prolific blooms for its small size. White and fragrant.

'Hermine' Star-shaped flowers that stand out of the water. Pointed petals; very free flowering.

'Lactae' Delicate pink blooms that fade to white as they age.

'Loose' The flowers are held 30cm (12in) above the water surface. Scented and star-shaped, often 15cm (6in) wide.

PINK AND RED BLOOMS

'Firecrest' Bright pink blooms with orange stamens with red tips.

odorata 'Turicensis' Medium-sized flowers of a soft deep pink. Fragrant with long and rounded petals.

odorata rosea Soft deep pink flowers of medium size, but the plant needs to spread in fairly shallow water and is often treated as a marginal.

'Pink Opal' Scented flowers of a pinky-red; the petals are broad and give a spectacular show.

'Rose Arey' Brilliant rose-pink blooms up to 20cm (8in) across with long pointed petals that are incurved. Free flowering and scented.

'Rose Magnolia' Delicate rose-pink blooms held above the water surface.

'Rose Nymph' Fragrant deep pink flowers that open 18cm (7in) wide.

'Somptuosa' One of the first water lilies to flower. Large semi-double rose-pink blooms that deepen to a deep strawberry pink in the centre.

RED BLOOMS

'Andreana' Large orange-red blooms. Free flowering with green leaves mottled with brown.

'Froebeli' Prolific wine-red flowers. A very reliable variety.

'Gloriosa' Bright red blooms. The growth rate and leaf area of this plant are minimal which, with its prolific flowering, makes it ideal for the smaller pond.

'James Brydon' Prolific bright red blooms. It will stand more shade than most water lilies and has a compact spread that makes it ideal for both

Below: 'Albatross', *a lovely white lily with a yellow centre; its young leaves will mature to bright green.*

small and medium-sized ponds. The leaves are purple to dark green
'Sanguinea' Blood-red flowers and leaves mottled brown on an olive green
'William Falconer' One of the darkest reds, with a yellow centre and a cup-shaped bloom. The foliage is dark green.
'Vesuve' Rich fire-red blooms.

YELLOW AND ORANGE BLOOMS
'Phoebus' Yellow blooms blushed with red and bright orange centres. The foliage is green and purple.

Left: 'Rose Nymph' *has large, beautiful rose-coloured blooms 18cm (7in) wide that are scented.*

Below: 'Gloriosa', *an ideal water lily for the smaller pond. It flowers for a long time with large fragrant blooms.*

'Robinsoniana' Orange-red flowers with lighter yellow-orange centres. The leaves are green heavily marked with purple.
'Sioux' The blooms open a buff-yellow and turn through peach to copper-orange as they age. The foliage is green mottled with brown.
'Solfatare' Star-shaped flowers of a warm yellow. The leaves are green marked with a deep brown-red.

STRIPED BLOOMS
'Darwin' A fragrant lily with red blooms strongly marked with white. The foliage is green.
'Eucharis' Deep pink flowers strikingly spotted and splashed with white.
'Livingstone' Deep cup-shaped scented blooms of red striped with white. Each flower has a deep brown-red centre making a compact shape.

Medium water lilies

These water lilies are suitable for medium-sized ponds. Allow 23-60cm (9-24in) of water over the crowns. The plants have a spread of about 90cm (3ft).

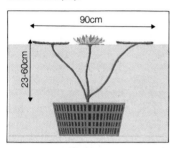

WHITE BLOOMS

'Gonnère' Also known as 'Crystal White' and 'Snowball', this is a semi-double with a profusion of white petals. The leaves are green.

'Hal Miller' Creamy white flowers held above the water surface.

odorata alba White heavily perfumed blooms. The plant prefers shallow water where it can spread.

'Tuberosa' Pure white flowers with golden centres. Apple-green foliage.

marliacea albida Pure white fragrant flowers with yellow centres. The leaves are green with smooth dark brown edges. Vigorous and free flowering, this is one of the most popular of all water lilies and the most widely planted.

PINK AND ROSE BLOOMS

'Amabilis' Flat star-shaped blooms of rose-pink, darkening as they age. Often up to 23cm (9in) across.

'Brackleyi Rosea' A scented lily of deep pink that fades with age. The free-flowering blooms stand just above the water level. It can occasionally seed itself.

'Fabiola' Rosy red flowers with a deep brown-red centre. The foliage is green.

'Jean de Lamarsalle' Pale pink blooms.

'Mme. Wilfron Gonnère' Double flowers of a rich pink, cup-shaped with the centre flushed rose. The leaves are plain green.

'Mrs. Richmond' Large blooms of deep pink, globe-like in shape with the colour becoming darker towards the centre.

marliacea carnea Also known as 'Morning Glory', this is a very popular plant with large fresh rose-pink blooms. Very free flowering with a vanilla fragrance. A robust plant.

marliacea rosea When this plant first flowers the blooms are barely pink but as it becomes established the colour becomes much stronger and deeper

Above: N. marliacea carnea, *also known as 'Morning Glory', is a very popular and robust water lily that* *flowers freely with large vanilla-scented fresh rose-pink blooms that are held above the water surface.*

towards the centre. Deeper in colour than marliacea carnea.

'Masaniello' Large flowers of rose deepening towards the centre and becoming darker as the plant matures. Free flowering with peony-shaped blooms.

'Rene Gerard' Red blooms streaked with pink becoming darker towards the centre and with pointed petals. The plant is free flowering but with less prolific leaf growth.

RED BLOOMS

'Attraction' Large flowers up to 25cm (10in) across of a garnet red flecked with white along the edges of the petals. Very free flowering, the young plants have pale pink blooms. Allow plenty of space as it is a vigorous grower.

'Bory de Saint Vincent' Well shaped strong red blooms. The foliage is a plain green.

'Conqueror' Large blooms that are blood red in the centre and have outer petals of a paler red with some white flecking. Often remains open in the evening.

'Escarboucle' A very popular water lily with large flat blooms of rich wine red with pointed petals. Very free flowering and of excellent quality. Well worth growing if you have space.

'Gloriosa' Red-rose blooms that change to deep rose, well scented and a prolific producer of flowers in a long season. Can be grown either in constricted areas or in a large pond.

marliacea rubra punctata Red flowers marked with lilac.

'Newton' Bowl-shaped blooms raised above the surface of the water, orange-red in colour with long gold stamens and pointed petals.

'Rene Gerard' Flowers with slender pointed petals of a rich rose streaked with crimson, becoming deeper towards the centre. Free flowering and with restricted leaf growth.

YELLOW BLOOMS

'Moorei' Pale yellow blooms up to 15cm (6in) wide, well proportioned and full petalled. The foliage is green with brown spots.

odorata sulphurea grandiflora The petals are narrow and plentiful, of a good pale yellow. The blooms are held above the water surface. The leaves are marked and spotted.

'Sunrise' Bright yellow delicately scented flowers with gold stamens held above the water surface. The foliage is dark green with red undersides marked in brown and is borne on hairy stems. Hardy but blooms much better under glass.

Above: 'Mme. Wilfron Gonnère' *has lovely double pink flowers, the petals often speckled with white.*

Above: 'Escarboucle' *has a very attractive bloom of deep red, with pointed petals; it is free flowering.*

Large water lilies

Water lilies for the larger pond that need 23cm-1.2m (9in-4ft) of water above the crown and will spread to over 1.2m (4ft) across.

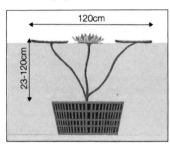

Above: 'Colossea', *a vigorous plant with large fragrant blooms, enjoys deep water and has a long season.*

WHITE BLOOMS

alba A vigorous water lily with white flowers 10-13cm (4-5in) across that is often used in areas of cold, deep and barely moving water where hybrids will not thrive. It quickly becomes established and spreads over a large area.

'Colossea' A plant for larger ponds as it is very vigorous with large scented white blooms. It has a long flowering period and will grow in deep water.

'Gladstoniana' Very large white flowers with golden centres. Needs deep water to expose the 20cm (8in) wide blooms.

tuberosa var. 'Richardsonii' Cup-shaped blooms held just above the water level with several rings of white petals round the centre of gold stamens. Needs deep water and can be vigorous.

'Virginalis' A white water lily with pointed petals regarded by some as the best shaped of all the whites. Free flowering through a long season.

PINK AND ROSE BLOOMS

'Baroness Orczy' Very large deep pink flowers.

'Formosa' Large rose-pink blooms that grow darker as they age, with gold stamens. Free flowering with green foliage.

'Leviathan' Large deep pink scented flowers.

'Mrs. C.W. Thomas' Semi-double pink scented blooms.

tuberosa rosea Scented blooms 10-13cm (4-5in) wide, pink and raised above the water surface. The foliage is light green and needs plenty of space to grow in width and depth.

RED BLOOMS

'Arethusa' Large globular flowers a deep dark red in the centre fading to deep rose on the outer petals.

atropurpurea Deep crimson to purple blooms about 20cm (8in) across that sit flat on the water surface and open wide to show off the long gold stamens in the centre. Free flowering. The young leaves are purple and mature to dark green.

'Attraction' A free-flowering water lily with deep garnet red blooms up to 25cm (10in) wide, the petals edged with white flecks. Young plants have pale pink blooms that suggest very little of the mature plant's potential. Provide space to show off the beauty of this popular hybrid.

'Charles de Meurville' Large blooms –up to 20cm (8in) wide – of a rich burgundy colour. The leaves are large and the plant needs plenty of space to grow well.

'Picciola' A vigorous lily with large dark crimson blooms about 25cm (10in) across that stand out of the water. The leaves are spotted and marked with dark red on green.

Right: Nymphaea marliacea chromatella, *a well-known yellow lily for the larger pond. It is free flowering.*

YELLOW AND ORANGE BLOOMS
'Colonel A.J. Welch' A water lily that is only recommended for deep water, which it stands better than marliacea chromatella. The yellow flowers are outweighed by the prolific leaves. The blooms stand well above the water surface. Faintly marbled foliage.
marliacea chromatella Large primrose yellow flowers 15-18cm (6-7in) across, full petalled and with

Above: 'Formosa' *has large rose-pink free-flowering blooms that darken with age and attractive gold stamens.*

good proportions. Reliably free flowering over a long season. The large green leaves are blotched with dark brown. The plant has been in cultivation for over a hundred years and is still very popular for the larger pond. A lovely water lily.

Bog plants

Stretches of open water are often surrounded by wetlands, areas of constantly moist soil where the water table is just beneath the surface. A number of plants have adapted their root system to cope with this high moisture level. Many of these 'bog plants' have brightly coloured flowers and interesting leaf shapes and make fine subjects for planting near a garden pond. Try growing some from the following selection.

Aconitum (1)
Monkshood; Wolf's Bane
Of this large family of plants, two are recommended: *A. carmichaelii* from Central China, 1.8m (6ft) tall with dark green foliage and blue flowers, and *A. napellus* from Europe and Asia, up to 1.2m (4ft) high with deeply cut leaves and violet-blue flowers. Increase by root division or by seed. Beware: all parts of the plant are poisonous.

Astilbe (2)
False Goat's Beard
A large group of plants from Europe and Asia. The most suitable ones are the *A. arendsii* hybrids, which bear white, pink, red and crimson blooms. The foliage is mid to deep green and deeply divided. The superb flowerheads are feathery and made up of tiny flowers. They appear throughout the summer months. Most of these plants will grow 60-90cm (2-3ft) high. Propagate astilbes by dividing the clumps in spring.

Camassia (3)
Quamash
A North American bulbous plant with sword-like leaves and spikes of purple, blue, white and cream flowers in early summer. A double variety is available. The plant grows to 90cm (3ft) tall and can be increased by division of the bulbs or by seed.

1   2   3   4

Claytonia (4)
Arctic Spring Beauty

A group of small plants from North America and Asia with fleshy rootstocks, smooth leaves and white or pink flowers in spring. *C. arctica*, *C. sibirica* and *C. virginica* all grow up to 15cm (6in) tall and thrive in peaty bog conditions. Increase by seed.

Eupatorium (5)
Hemp Agrimony

A large family from the Northern Hemisphere comprising shrubby and herbaceous plants with varying leaves and large heads of daisy-like flowers in white, pink and purple from midsummer until early autumn. Usually growing up to 1.2m (4ft) tall some, such as *E. cannabinum*, can reach 1.8m (6ft) in a rich and moist soil. Cut the stems almost to ground level after flowering and increase by dividing the rootstock.

Filipendulina (6)
Dropwort

From Europe, Asia and North America, these plants are like *Spiraea*, to which they are closely related. They have long green leaves in a variety of shapes, mainly lobed, and large heads of small white, pink or red flowers. Some varieties can reach 2.4m (8ft) tall, but most grow to 90cm (3ft). Increase by root division.

Gunnera manicata (7)
A striking Brazilian plant that looks like a giant rhubarb. The leaves can reach 3m (10ft) long by 2.4m (8ft) wide and the flowers are like long circular brushes 1m (3.3ft) tall. Frost will cut the foliage back, but if the crown is covered with a layer of leaves or bracken it will survive the winter. The plant can reach 4.5m (15ft) high and 6m (20ft) wide, making it suitable only for the larger garden. Divide plants.

5   6   7

Helonius bullata
Swamp Pink; Stud Flower
A North American plant with shiny leaves clustered in rosettes and spikes of pink flowers in spring. It grows up to 45cm (18in) tall and has a tuberous rooted system that can be divided for increasing stock.

Heloniopsis
Two Japanese spring-flowering plants, *H. breviscarpa* with white flowers and *H. japonica* with pink blooms, are recommended. Both have spear-shaped leaves and should reach 30cm (12in) tall in a good moist soil. *H. breviscarpa* sometimes increases by producing small plants on its leaf ends; otherwise divide the rootstock.

Hemerocallis (1)
Day Lily
The best of this group of plants come from China. They have sword-like leaves and many hybrids are available to provide a wide range of midsummer colour. They will reach 60-107cm (2-3.5ft) tall and can be increased by root division in spring.

Hosta (3)
Funkia
Most hostas originate in Japan and are grown for their fine decorative foliage and their ability to thrive in shade. The leaves are veined and are available in blue, yellow, green and variegations. The flower spikes, white or mauve in colour, appear in early summer. Plants grow to 75cm (30in) in height. Increase by division in the spring. Guard against slug damage.

Iris (4)
A large group of plants containing some species that thrive in moist conditions. Most come from China and have sword-like leaves and fine iris blooms, some heavily marked and

1   2   3   4

veined. Recommended are: *Iris bulleyana*, *I. chrysographes*, *I. forestii*, *I. kaempferi*, *I. laevigata*, *I. sibirica* and *I. wilsonii*. *I. kaempferi* needs to be kept dry during the winter months. Normally increased by division. (See also description of irises under 'Deep water and marginal plants' page 58.)

Ligularia (5)
Mainly of Chinese and Japanese origin, most ligularias have heart-shaped leaves and spikes of yellow and orange daisy-like flowers in summer. They can thrive in a deep moist soil and can reach 1.5m (5ft) tall. Increase by division in spring.

Lobelia (2)
A few of the American members of this family will thrive by the pond: *L. cardinalis*, with oblong leaves and spikes of red flowers; *L. fulgens* and its hybrids, with purple and red foliage; and *L. syphilitica*, with blue or white flowers. All grow up to 90cm (3ft) tall and can be increased by root division during the spring.

Lysichitum (6)
Two spring-flowering plants, *L. americanum* from America, with large yellow flowers and pointed green leaves, and *L. camschatense* from Japan, with white flowers like the Arum Lily can be recommended. They are easily grown in either shallow water or wet soil, in sun or partial shade. Up to 90cm (3ft) tall and easily raised from seed.

Primulas (7)
Most of the moisture-loving primulas come from Eastern Asia and have a variety of forms; the flowers can be single or in umbels of up to 50 blooms in a variety of colours. Some will reach up to 90cm (3ft) tall while others will only make 15cm (16in) in height. They can be grown from seed or division.

5   6   7

---------- **PART 4** ----------

POND FISH

No matter how beautiful a pond and its surroundings may be, there's always a sense of disappointment if, on looking into its depths, there are no fish to be seen. To most pondkeepers, a pond is not complete without the orange-red snout of a goldfish peeping out from beneath the edge of a water-lily pad, the occasional muted splash as a Golden Orfe leaps over the surface or a shoal of majestic Koi cruises around in formation. Keeping fish in the pond has practical value too: although no longer stocked for food, pond fishes perform a valuable service in keeping down mosquito, gnat and midge populations by eating the waterborne larval stage of these troublesome insects.

Take great care when choosing different types of fish for your pond. We have already seen that the environmental conditions in some types of pond are not universally suitable for all fish; apart from their different basic needs, certain collections of fishes won't even look right together. Koi, for instance, are 'restless' fish, constantly swimming around the pond; once they get to any appreciable size, their very bulk and passage through the water will set up currents that may well be unsettling to smaller, more sedentary fishes. Also, at feeding times small fishes often lose out, being literally left behind in the rush for food. Orfe are active fishes and, like many native fishes, appreciate well oxygenated, and even running water. Native fishes, although often readily available for pond culture, and able to thrive in such conditions, are sometimes too drab in colour to be noticed – hardly recommended decorative additions – although some North American species are an exception. Native fishes need to be chosen with care, for many will outgrow the pond and some become predaceous.

The pond can also be used as a seasonal home (during summer months) for other fishes; these include the more delicate Fancy Goldfish varieties and also some 'tropical' species, more used to warmer waters. However, this use is better restricted to small ponds in which the water warms up quickly, and re-catching in autumn is that much easier.

Right: *These prize fish explain the fascination that koi hold for many pondkeepers.*

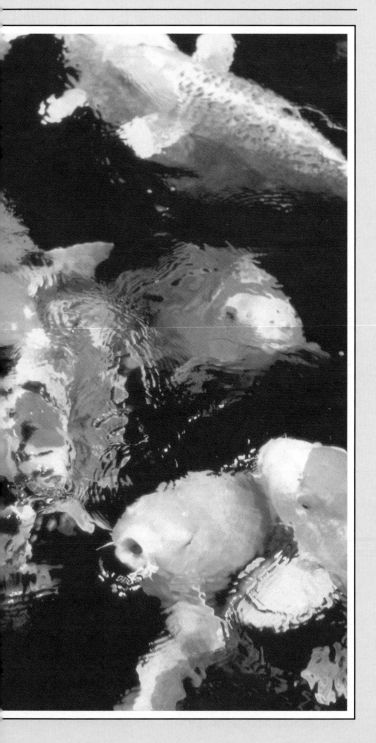

Selecting and transporting fish

As you will see in the later sections of this book, there is a wide selection of fish suitable for the pond; although this wide-ranging choice might seem confusing, the principles involved in choosing which particular fish to buy apply equally to all, with only a few extra cautions for some species.

When to buy
Generally, new ponds are installed between late spring and early autumn when the weather is likely to be settled long enough for the sometimes lengthy construction process; there are also good fishkeeping reasons for this. After spring, the water temperature rises, and fish awakening from winter torpor are more lively, with healthy appetites and consequent faster growing rates. If the fish can become well-established in the pond throughout the summer months, when an abundance of natural foods is available, by the time autumn comes they should be well prepared to face the winter months, relying on previously

accumulated fatty reserves. Autumn is generally the time for cleaning a pond before winter, and a renovated pond might not be re-established enough to keep any recently introduced fishes in good condition. Introducing fish in very early spring may also be unsatisfactory for the same reason.

Choosing healthy stock
You cannot expect a fish to thrive in captivity, however excellent its living conditions, if it is sickly or below standard quality to begin with. Before selecting individual fishes, you will need to find a good-quality retail outlet to supply your fishes. Ideally, choose a local supplier – the water quality is more likely to be the same as yours (probably supplied by the same water company) and the journey home will be shorter, which will minimize stress to the fishes in transit. On balance it is usually best to go to a specialist fish retail outlet, where advice is usually sound, being based on experience. (Some garden centre staff may not

Above: Netting a Koi for closer inspection at a show. The fishes are usually displayed in a blue plastic basket that floats in the water.

Above: Small Koi for sale at a show. Fish of this size are ideal for beginners setting up a pond.

Left: Koi held in pens at a Koi farm in Japan. The netting is used to provide vital shade to prevent fish literally becoming 'sun burnt'.

be quite so well versed or experienced in aquatic matters.)

Observe the fish in their display tanks and ponds carefully. Avoid choosing a fish from any display that contains ailing, or even dead, fish, no matter how healthy the one you have picked out appears to be; it may well already be infected. The fish's body should be neither too thin nor too fat: a very thin body may be the result of internal disease, and no amount of good feeding will restore the fish to full health. A bloated body, especially when accompanied by sticking out scales, is also a sign of disease. (However, a fish that looks plump when viewed from above may simply be a female in spawning condition – and it may be difficult to spot the difference!)

Try to get a really good look at the fish you want to buy – not always easy if the fish are kept in a pond or large vats: small fish are fairly easy to scrutinize at close quarters (in a plastic bag after being caught); large Koi are a different matter. They should be netted, and brought to the side of the pool without being lifted from the water; at the poolside they can then be transferred into shallow bowls or perforated plastic crates for closer examination.

If the fish are kept in an eye-level tank it will be much easier to examine them for other physical defects. Any fish with split fins, protruding eyes (unless a characteristic of the strain, such as Telescope-eyed Fancy Goldfish, which are not really hardy enough for keeping in a pond), obvious wounds, pimples, spots or ulcers must be rejected out of hand. The fish's skin should be clear – any opacity in the protective mucus (or over-production of mucus itself) should be viewed with suspicion.

A fish's behaviour is also a good guide to its health; it should be swimming and breathing easily, without effort, with all fins erect – hanging at the surface, an inability to remain still at any chosen level or lying on the pond floor are all signs of ill-health.

You may be buying fish not only for decorative purposes but also for breeding stock; here you will be looking for other factors in addition to basic good health. Most pond fish can be bred selectively (as well as spawning spontaneously among themselves), which means that the fishkeeper is able to put together fish that have all the desirable qualities between them. When choosing fish from which to breed, you will need to pay closer attention to details such as colour pattern definition, colour intensity, finnage, and adherence to recognized show standards.

Many ornamental fishes are imported from abroad – Koi are a notable example, coming from Israel, America, Singapore or Europe as well as their usual country of origin, Japan. Depending on source, the quality of the fish may vary in accordance with the price.

How many fish?
Various equations exist to work out how many fish a pond will hold – 'body-lengths per volume of water' is one method. A more commonly used guide is 'body-lengths per unit of surface area', where the oxygen intake capability of the pond is taken into account. Two ponds of the same surface area may well have differing volumes of water, yet their oxygen intake area is the same – the fish just have more room to swim about in the deeper pond.

A reasonable guide is to allow 15cm (6in) of body length (excluding the tail) for each 1800cm^2 (2ft^2) of surface area. This gives more than adequate room for growth. Unfortunately this rule is not totally flexible, as a single large fish will consume more oxygen than an equivalent total body length of smaller ones. Further complications in these calculations are caused by the fact that any water-circulation systems (filters, fountains, waterfalls etc) aerate the water even more, thus allowing greater numbers of fish to be supported, although in summer any increase in temperature actually lowers the oxygen content. It comes down to personal preference in the end, but 20 large fish are more visible than 100 small ones, especially in a large pond. Once you have arrived at a theoretical total fish population, do not buy sufficient fish to meet this limit right at the outset. Any new pond will take some months to find its internal 'balance', as will the filtration system, and initial overstocking will soon lead to fish losses.

Transporting fish

Small to medium-sized fish can be transported quite satisfactorily in plastic bags of suitable sizes. If the journey is to be long – you may see fish for sale during a day out, for instance, or even have made a special journey to buy fish – then it is usual practice for some extra oxygen to be put into the bag. Large fish, such as Koi, can be moved in stouter plastic bags

Below and right: Oxygen is added to the bag to sustain the fish on the journey home (below). Once inflated, the bag is tied at the neck. Float the bag on the surface of your quarantine pond for at least an hour before release (right).

(often triple-bagged for safety), in expanded polystyrene (styrofoam) boxes, which hold water remarkably well, or in plastic dustbins. The fish will suffer less travel-stress if its bag is covered; a blanket will not only restrict light but also protect the plastic bag against accidental damage. A battery-operated air-pump can be used to supply aeration, especially during long journeys if the weather is hot; where extra oxygen is not available, frequent stops to open the containers and admit air may also be advisable.

The risk of thermal shock, when eventually introducing fish into the pond, can be minimized by floating the 'carry-home' plastic bags in the pond for an hour or two until the two water temperatures equalize, at which time the fish can be gently released.

Feeding fish

Despite the added seasonal elements to the fish's diet that natural, water-borne crustaceans and insects bring, pond fish (like aquarium fish) depend on their owner to provide them with a correct balanced diet. This is just as vital for the hardy Goldfish as for Koi, which need a twice-yearly change of diet (see page 128). In addition to providing the fish with energy, adequate growth and natural repair facilities of body tissues, a balanced diet improves resistance to disease, enhances coloration and promotes successful reproduction.

Both Goldfish and Koi are omnivores, so care must be taken to include food of both animal and vegetables in their diet.

Providing a balanced diet

A balanced diet should consist of proteins, fat or oils, carbohydrates, fibre, minerals, vitamins and trace elements, all present in the correct amounts. Too little or too much of certain nutrients can lead to problems.

Let us look at these basic 'ingredients' in more detail.

Proteins are complex nitrogen-containing compounds that are essential for the growth of young fish and for the repair of worn out tissues. These may be supplied from animal (e.g. fish meal) or plant (e.g. soya meal) sources, although it is easier for some fish to digest the former. Since fish cannot store protein in their bodies for use when supplies are short, it is important that the diet contains adequate amounts at all times. Proprietary fish foods vary in their protein content; it is typically 20-45%. Actively growing fish fry will require a diet containing a higher proportion of protein than slower growing or adult fish, so you should choose the food accordingly to allow for this.

The quality as well as the quantity of the protein is also important. Proteins are made up of a number of amino acids, some of which must be in the diet at all

times. Even if a diet contains large amounts of protein but the protein is lacking in certain amino acids, nutritional disorders may develop. To help counteract this problem, the diet should include protein from a wide selection of sources. The good-quality flaked and other dried foods are suitable in this respect.

Fats or oils and carbohydrates are available from a wide variety of sources. They are important energy-producing foods. However, in contrast to protein, if a diet is too rich in these nutrients, the excess may be stored within the body of the fish. In extreme cases, this can have serious side-effects.

Fibre forms quite a large part of the diet for many omnivorous and herbivorous fish. In commercially prepared foods, it may also be used to add bulk to a diet that might otherwise be too concentrated and, perhaps, wasteful in use.

Vitamins, minerals and trace elements need only be present in relatively small amounts, although they are essential for a healthy balanced diet. Many fresh foods are a good source of these nutrients, as are high-quality prepared fish diets.

Proprietary foods

Today, a range of proprietary diets and other foods are available for all kinds of aquarium fish, including goldfish. These 'manufactured' foods can be broadly classified as dried, freeze-dried and frozen.

Dried foods such as flakes, pellets, sticks and tablets, are widely available and are convenient to use. If you buy good-quality brands, these can form the basis of the diet. The special goldfish foods available are ideal, but avoid using foods based largely upon biscuit meal, ants eggs and the like since they generally have a low nutritional value compared to other types.

Many types of dried foods, especially flaked foods, feature special 'growth', 'colour' and 'vegetable' diets. Even though these may have been developed for tropical fish, their occasional use will add valuable variety to the goldfish diet.

Most dried foods have a limited shelf life and generally they should be used within a few months of purchase. Although they can still be used after this period, the vitamin levels decrease with time. Bulk buying of flaked foods, therefore, can sometimes be a false saving.

Freeze-dried and frozen fish diets are also available from aquarium shops. Although these have been developed primarily for tropical and marine fish, they are also useful for adding variety to the diet of goldfish and for conditioning brood fish for breeding. Convenient freeze-dried foods include *Tubifex* worms, mosquito larvae, bloodworms, *Daphnia* (water fleas) and brineshrimp (*Artemia salina*).

Live foods
A number of live foods can be used to add variety to the diet and to condition fish for breeding. However, their use brings with it a number of potential dangers. To begin with, feeding a restricted range of live foods, to the exclusion of all other kinds of foods, is unlikely to provide a balanced diet, and may even lead to nutritional or other internal disorders for the fish. Do not, therefore, totally replace good-quality dried foods with live food. Furthermore, as many live foods originate from ponds, streams or rivers, they may bring with them aquarium pests, such as *Hydra* or snails, or even fish disease organisms. The risk of introducing disease organisms can be reduced by collecting live foods from fish-free water, but the possibility of introducing aquarium pests still remains. It may be safer to use live foods that do not live in water.

Here, we consider a range of live foods and discuss their merits and possible drawbacks in relation to pond fish.

Earthworms Earthworms are the easiest live food to obtain. They can be collected by the dozen at night, especially after rain. All you need is a flashlight and a quick hand. Undisturbed, the worms will remain above ground but quickly retreat into their holes when they sense danger. Another way of collecting worms is to lay a hessian sack in a shady corner of the garden. Place a layer of tea leaves underneath it and keep them wet. The worms will accumulate under the hessian and provide you with a steady supply. It is also possible to breed them in large wooden boxes filled with earth. Feed them with vegetable refuse, such as potato peelings and

Above: *Don't be fooled by the greedy appetites of Koi, in particular; overfeeding your fish will quickly pollute the pond.*

cabbage leaves. If worm-collecting does not appeal to you, there are companies that specialize in breeding worms for the coarse-fishing market and will sell them in small tubs.

Earthworms are an excellent live food. The small ones can be fed whole, while larger specimens can be cut up before feeding them to the fish. They are easily digestible.

Daphnia These small crustaceans ('water fleas') can be bought from aquatic or pet stores or you can collect them in warm weather from ponds, especially those used by cattle. *Daphnia* swim with a jerky motion and are easy to catch with a fine mesh net. The problem with obtaining *Daphnia* from a wild source is that they may carry parasites and diseases into the

Below and below right: *These panels show a selection of suitable foods for goldfishes. Use them sparingly to provide a varied diet.*

pond. While it is possible to breed *Daphnia*, most people find it too troublesome. Obtained from a reliable, disease-free source, *Daphnia* are an excellent food source for fry and young fish, but will be consumed just as readily by adult Koi in the pond.

Tubifex worms These aquatic worms are bright red in colour and up to 5cm (2in) long. They are sold by weight in aquatic stores. In their natural state they live in the mud around sewerage outlets. To avoid introducing disease into the pond, wash worms from a suspect source thoroughly in clean water for several days to evacuate their intestines before feeding them to the fish. To keep *Tubifex* worms alive, place them in a shallow dish under a constantly dripping tap.

Bloodworms These larval stages of midges are blood red in colour and jointed. They swim in a characteristic sideways motion and

DRIED FOODS

◄**Pellets** Wide range that float or sink.

◄**Foodsticks** Longer pellets that float.

Tablets Both ► sinking and stick-on types.

◄**Flakes** Well-balanced staple diet.

Notes: High-quality dried foods can provide the basic diet.

FREEZE-DRIED AND FROZEN FOODS

◄ **Water fleas** Convenient freeze-dried form.

Bloodworms ► Larval midges, nutritious food.

Krill Marine shrimp. ► Best supplied in freeze-dried form.

Shrimps Smaller ► kinds can be fed in frozen form.

◄ **Tubifex cubes** Can be stuck on glass at any level.

◄ **Mosquito larvae** Excellent for conditioning fishes.

Notes: The benefits of live foods without the risk of disease.

reach up to 12mm (0.5in) in length. They provide a nutritious live food.

Mosquito larvae These will be found during the warmer months in any stagnant water, such as a rainwater butt. They 'breathe' through the rear part of the body and hang upside-down from the water surface. They are black and usually about 1cm (0.4in) in length, although there are several species and the larvae vary in size. They may be caught with a fine-mesh net and will be greedily accepted by all fish.

Glassworms These transparent larvae – also called Phantom Larvae – float horizontally in the water and move with sharp twisting movements. They may be 1cm (0.4in) long, and again are eagerly sought after by most fishes.

Maggots These are obtainable from fishing tackle shops. Be sure to choose only the white ones and do not buy any that have been dyed.

Water lice These are common in both still and flowing waters and resemble woodlice in appearance. Koi eat them with relish, although only the larger fish seem able to cope with their hard carapace, or outer shell.

Tadpoles If frogs spawn in your pool, the Koi will eat the tadpoles enthusiastically, although they appear to ignore those of the toad.

Plants Softer-leaved oxygenating plants may be nibbled by Goldfish (Koi will eat them whole, along with duckweed!), but marginals and water lilies usually remain untouched by all fishes.

Household food
With the development of commercial fish food, the need to offer fishes kitchen scraps and other household foods has all but disappeared. Nevertheless, some fishkeepers continue to feed their fish tinned peas, other vegetables,

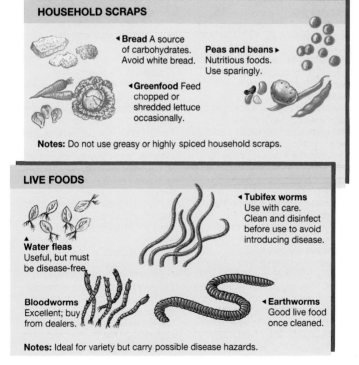

HOUSEHOLD SCRAPS

◄**Bread** A source of carbohydrates. Avoid white bread.

Peas and beans ► Nutritious foods. Use sparingly.

◄**Greenfood** Feed chopped or shredded lettuce occasionally.

Notes: Do not use greasy or highly spiced household scraps.

LIVE FOODS

Water fleas Useful, but must be disease-free.

◄**Tubifex worms** Use with care. Clean and disinfect before use to avoid introducing disease.

Bloodworms Excellent; buy from dealers.

◄**Earthworms** Good live food once cleaned.

Notes: Ideal for variety but carry possible disease hazards.

brown bread, etc., claiming that this is not only economical, but also of great benefit to the fish. Exercise care, however, to ensure that such foods are eaten and digested by the fish and are not allowed to pollute the pond.

Guidelines for feeding goldfish
During most of the year, you should feed goldfish two or three times a day with as much food as they will consume in a few minutes. You should soon be able to gauge the amount of food required. If you give too much food, the excess may accumulate, decay and cause water quality problems. Each time you offer food, the fish should rise eagerly to the water surface. If not, this may indicate that they have been overfed, or that there is some other problem in the pond.

Goldfish are 'cold-blooded' and take their body temperature from the surrounding water. This means that at higher temperatures they will be more active and require more food than at lower temperatures. The appetite of goldfish will decrease significantly as water temperatures fall below 12°C (54°F), and very little food will be required below 8-10°C (46-50°F).

As already mentioned, good-quality dried foods can form a staple diet for goldfish. However, two or three times a week, it is a good idea to offer a little freeze-dried, frozen or live food to add variety to the diet and help condition the fish, especially for breeding. The conditioning of adult fish for breeding and the foods needed for rearing the fry are discussed in more detail in the section starting on page 46.

Remember that many dried foods contain only about 10% water and are thus more concentrated than frozen or live foods, which may contain 70-80% water. This means that fish require surprisingly small amounts of dried food in order to remain healthy. It is also much easier to pollute the aquarium with dried foods than when using frozen or live foods.

Above: *Feeding Koi with floating pellets. These fishes are about 10cm (4in) long and are eagerly taking the 'mini' pellets. Use pellets as the basic food for Koi, with additional live foods to provide a balanced diet.*

Guidelines for feeding Koi
Always feed your Koi in the same place. In this way, they will become very tame and learn to eat from your hand. By bringing the fish in close, you can monitor them for any loss of condition or disease. You will also notice if any of them are missing, which may give you warning that there are hungry herons about.

It is better to underfeed rather than overfeed. Because Koi do not have an organ equivalent to a stomach, they cannot eat a great quantity of food at one time. Therefore, stick to the rule of feeding them 'little and often'. Feeding too much also increases the danger of polluting the pool with uneaten food.

It is normal practice to feed Koi twice a day. For the first meal in the morning, give them an easily

digestible food that is high in carbohydrates. The second feed should be in the afternoon or evening and should contain more protein than carbohydrate.

Processed foods Koi are omnivorous and eat a wide variety of foods. Most people use proprietary brands of food, which are generally available as pellets. These are produced in different grades to suit Koi at various sizes, from pellets 1.5mm (0.06in) in diameter for fishes between 5 and 10cm (2-4in) long, to 7mm (0.3in) pellets for fishes over 30cm (12in) long. Standard food contains protein (usually fish-based) plus a mixture of vitamins and minerals. Other processed foods contain vegetable-based protein, such as wheatgerm meal, plus *Spirulina platensis*, a high nutritious species of filamentous alga from Mexico. *Spirulina* is quickly digested, and thus can be fed at quite low temperatures. It also acts as a 'colour' food, serving to strengthen and 'fix' the coloured areas of the fish. Other pellets may contain carotene, which also acts as an effective colour enhancer.

Pellets may be of the floating or sinking variety. The latter are best for the cooler months, when Koi are not so active.

As water temperatures fall, the Koi's ability to digest protein declines and so an autumnal change in diet to one containing a higher content of vegetable matter (such as wheatgerm) is recommended to enable the fish to build up necessary reserves for over-wintering, during which time no food will be taken.

Iroage This Japanese term describes the practice of bring out the best colour potential of your Koi. By caring for the fish in certain ways, and by feeding certain foods, their colour pigments can be enhanced Iroage foods may contain dried shrimps and algae such as *Chiorella* and *Spirulina*. Always use these foods as directed. If used to excess, *Chlorella* may make the white areas of the fish take on a reddish tinge, for example.

Fish anatomy

Until you start keeping fishes you may well think that one fish looks exactly like another, but very soon you will find out that there are many variations on the standard shape. Each variation has evolved over many years and generations of fishes, as Nature constantly refines the design, which is adapted to suit the fish's environment and feeding style.

A fish with a large body surface area is suitable for only slow-running or still waters; it could not cope with strong water currents. A fat cylindrical fish would not be at home among dense reed-beds, where a slim species would be. An upturned mouth is ideal for taking food from the water surface, but not from the river floor. Barbels (complete with taste-sensing cells) around the underslung mouth of a bottom-dwelling fish, coupled with large eyes, enable the animal to find its food in dark muddy waters and to be aware of any predators lurking close by.

Scales

Scales provide streamlining and protection for the body against injury. They grow constantly as the fish matures, and growth in a fish can be determined by noting the extra rings around each scale. However, these rings are not necessarily annual growth rings as with a tree, but are dependent on the seasons and the supply of food.

Fins

Fins are used for locomotion and stability, and, in some fishes, as spawning aids, either in courtship ritual displays or as egg-carriers, reproductive organs or water impellers over deposited eggs.

Generally, fishes have seven fins: three single and two pairs. The *anal* fin and *dorsal* fin act as stabilizers, and some species, such as the Perch *(Perca fluviatilis)*, may have two dorsal fins. The tail or *caudal* fin provides the main forward thrust to drive the fish through the water. The paired *pelvic*, or *ventral*, and *pectoral* fins are used for manoeuvring, braking and adjusting the position of the fish in the water in much the same way as the hydroplanes on a submarine. They may also be used to perform fanning duties for removing dirt from eggs. The *pelvic* fins of some bottom-dwelling fishes are fused together to form a suction cup that prevents the fish from being swept away by water currents. In some tropical fishes there is an extra fin found between the dorsal and the caudal fin; this is the

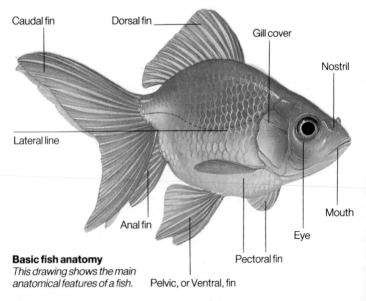

Basic fish anatomy
This drawing shows the main anatomical features of a fish.

Caudal fin · Dorsal fin · Gill cover · Nostril · Lateral line · Anal fin · Pectoral fin · Eye · Mouth · Pelvic, or Ventral, fin

Above: *This blue Japanese carp has little guanin below the skin but has retained a line of sparkling scales.*

adipose fin, a small fatty tissue structure, the purpose of which is not clear. Most fins are supported by hard rays, and in many instances the male can erect its dorsal fin at will to display to the female of the species or to threaten rival males.

Fishes cultivated in the aquarium and the pond often have exaggerated finnage, developed by intensively controlled selective breeding programmes; such finnage would not be found on fishes in the wild state, as the extra-long flowing fins would be more of a hindrance to the fish than an advantage.

Senses
The fish has the same five senses that we enjoy, although it differs in that its nostrils are used solely for smelling and not for breathing. Fishes can hear, but they also have the ability to sense very low frequency vibrations in the water by means of their *lateral line* system; this can be seen as a row of tiny holes in the scales along the sides of the fish, and vibrations are detected by the nervous system connected to these holes. Whisker-like growths called *barbels* are often found around the mouth in bottom-dwelling species and these help the fish to detect its food by taste rather than by sight.

Swim-bladder
Most fishes have a hydrostatic buoyancy organ that automatically adjusts itself to give the fish neutral density, and so allows it to remain at any chosen depth in the water.

Colour
Fishes use colour in many ways: it may attract a mate, assist in species recognition, or be a very useful means of camouflage; it may even be used as a warning to other fishes to keep off; and it certainly attracts fishkeepers. Colour is produced in the fish in two ways: by reflection and by pigmentation.

Colour produced by reflection relies on *guanin,* a waste substance that is not excreted from the body but stored just beneath the skin, forming a light-reflecting layer. What colour light is reflected, ie what colour the fish presents to us, depends on how the crystals of guanin are aligned.

In Goldfishes, this layer of guanin may be present to give the familiar metallic look; or it may lie deeper in the skin, giving the impression that the fish has a mother-of-pearl sheen; or it may be lacking altogether, giving a matt finish.

Colour due to pigmentation can also lie at various depths in the skin; and the combinations of pigmentation hues with the three 'finishes' described above (to say nothing of the finnage development possibilities) give very ample scope for genetic experimentation in Goldfish breeding. Fishes can alter the apparent distribution of pigmentation, and at times the colours may be heightened or faded depending on their mood. As one would expect, the onset of breeding will be signalled by the intensifying of colour and the displaying of fins. An extra clue to the imminence of breeding is the development of small white pimples (tubercles) on the pectoral fins and gill plates of the male fishes, often mistaken as disease symptoms by some fishkeepers.

As with other fishes, variation in the colour and patterning of Koi is caused both by the amount and position of reflective guanin in the skin and by the presence of true pigments. The many colours and patterns of Koi are recognized internationally by their Japanese names. Although at first difficult to grasp, these names are built up logically from simple terms that denote colour, pattern, resemblance to natural forms, and also reference to the periods of history in which they were developed. The different Koi varieties available and the names used to describe them are featured on page 170-209.

Gills and respiration
Beneath the gill cover, or operculum, on each side of the head are four gill arches. Each gill arch supports a large number of finger-like gill filaments. Water is taken in through the mouth and forced over the gill filaments and out via the raised gill covers. As the water passes over the gill filaments, the fine blood vessels they contain absorb oxygen and release waste products such as carbon dioxide and ammonia. This process of gaseous exchange is similar to the process that occurs in the lungs of an air-breathing animal.

Since fish are 'cold-blooded' (more correctly known as poikilothermic or ectothermic), their body temperature fluctuates with that of the environment and they are more active – and thus require more oxygen – at higher temperatures. However, because warmer water frequently contains less oxygen than cool water, fish will show increased gill movements in warm, poorly aerated water.

Feeding and digestion
The downturned mouth of the goldfish indicates a tendency to feed at the bottom of the pond, although fishes will also feed at the water surface. Goldfish and Koi do not have teeth in their mouths, however. They feed by taking food

in and then crushing it using the pharyngeal teeth at the back of the throat. The number and shape of pharyngeal teeth is useful in identifying certain members of the carp family. Unfortunately, they can only be examined in dead fish.

Digestive system
The goldfish, like many other members of the carp family, feeds on both animal and plant material. Its relatively long intestine helps the fish to digest plant material. By comparison, more carnivorous fish have much shorter intestines. There is no well-defined stomach in the goldfish, but more of a gradual change in appearance and function along the length of the alimentary tract.

Food taken into the mouth is crushed by the pharyngeal teeth, and passes into the first part of the alimentary tract. Here digestion begins, with the help of digestive juices and enzymes secreted by the fish. Once digestion is well under way, the products of this process are absorbed through the alimentary tract wall into the bloodstream and distributed around the body. The indigestible material passes along the alimentary tract and out into the water via the vent.

Since the body temperature of a goldfish is similar to that of its surroundings, the fish feeds more actively at higher water temperatures, while at lower temperatures it becomes dormant and its appetite wanes. Fishes can go for long periods without food and will come to no harm; in cold water they may cease to feed altogether.

Kidneys
In their freshwater environment, water is continually being drawn into the body tissues of goldfishes and, as a result, they rarely need to drink. However, the fish has to get rid of the excess water in its body and this process is carried out by the kidneys. These are situated beneath the backbone and run along the length of the body. They

Above: *The paired pectoral and pelvic fins are used for making precise movements, the tail fin provides thrust, and the dorsal and anal fins give the fish stability.*

produce large amounts of dilute urine, which also contains salts and other waste products.

Reproductive organs
The reproductive organs – testes in the male, ovaries in the female – are situated just below the swimbladder. At breeding time these organs swell and give the fish, notably the female, a very rounded appearance. The male stimulates the female to shed her eggs into the water, where he fertilizes them with his milt, or sperm. Fertilization is thuys external. (See pages 152-157.)

Size and life expectancy
There are many tales of the family pet goldfish living for many years (often under the most adverse conditions in undersized indoor aquariums), and lengths of 20-25cm (8-10in) at 5-6 years of age are normal. Specimens up to 30cm (12in) long and weighing 4.5kg (10lb) have been recorded.

In ideal conditions in Japan, Koi have grown to more than 95cm (37.5in) in length and it is quite possible for Koi to reach 70cm (27.5in) in good conditions elsewhere. Life expectancy varies widely depending on individual circumstances; 'Hanako', the oldest Koi in Japan, was reputed to have lived for more than 200 years. Kept in the right conditions, it is possible for Koi to achieve a lifespan of 60 years.

Fish health

The first signs of disease in a fish are usually pretty obvious. A keen fishkeeper can tell a sick fish from a distance, just by its attitude in the water. The fish looks rather miserable and often listless, with folded fins and a lack-lustre look to the body. Other signs include gasping at the surface and quick darting movements, often accompanied by the fish attempting to scrape itself against planting baskets and other hard surfaces.

You are most likely to encounter disease among your stock a short period after purchase. This is because the majority of diseases are triggered by stress. Most Koi are imported and the handling, netting, travelling and overcrowding, together with fluctuating temperatures and water changes, are all obviously upsetting to the fish. This stress often leads to loss of condition and a reduced ability to resist infection. For this reason, it is extremely important to quarantine newly acquired fish.

Fish disease is a complex and wide-ranging subject. Here, we consider a selection of the most common diseases and health problems your pond fish may encounter. Many other bacterial, parasitic and organic disorders, such as tumours, are common. In many cases, diagnosis without laboratory facilities is impossible.

Before we look at the infections we consider briefly the types of treatment possible.

Methods of treatment

Treatment methods vary according to the disease or problem being tackled, ranging from simply adding

Basic treatment techniques

Above: *These photographs show treatment of an individual fish. These techniques should be undertaken only by a veterinarian or suitably qualified or experienced* *fishkeepers. Once anaesthetized, this Koi has been laid on a wet towel. Folding the corners of the towel over the head and tail will keep it calm and secure.*

a treatment to the water to delicate surgical techniques that can only be performed by a veterinarian.

Medicated bath Some treatments involve immersing the fish for a short period of, say, 5 minutes, while others take longer. Various chemicals and drugs are added to the water in specific concentrations. Sometimes the fish are removed from the pool for a short bath in the solution. In many cases this is not practical and the whole pond is dosed. This process is repeated until a cure is effected. When adding treatments directly to the pond, it is essenbtial to know the volume of water accurately to calculate the dosage.

Oral administration Antibiotics and other specific medicines are often mixed with food in order to combat various bacterial ailments.

Surface painting This is chiefly used to treat wounds and lesions, but also for body ulcers. In these cases, compounds such as mercurochrome, methylene blue or povidone-iodine are painted on with a fine brush or cotton bud.

Injections These are only used when treating large and valuable fish and should be administered by a veterinarian. Generally, antibiotics are used in the treatment of bacterial infections. Possible injection sites are the muscles behind the pectoral fin and the area behind the vent.

Surgery This is only performed by veterinarians on large and valuable fish, generally to remove tumours.

Above: *Cleaning the site of damage with a cotton bud. This is the first stage of any course of treatment, particularly for wounds and lesions.*

Above: *Applying mercurochrome (or an equivalent preparation such as povidone-iodine) to sterilize. Use mercurochrome with care.*

Above: *Applying a waterproof ointment to the site as the final stage of treatment. Such ointments adhere well to the skin and kill bacteria in the region of the wound.*

Above: *Injecting a Koi, in this case with a general purpose antibiotic. If you are not experienced, ask your veterinarian or local dealer to carry out such specialized tasks.*

HINTS FOR TREATING POND FISH

1 It is usually safer and easier to treat diseased fish in an aquarium than in the pond, especially where one may need individual attention. Calculating the volume of water is important for administering correct dosages of medication and this is obviously much easier to do accurately in a hospital tank than in an irregularly shaped, varying depth pond.

2 Calculate the volume of the tank or bowl carefully. Tank length x width x water depth (measured in cm) and divided by 1000 equals the volume in litres. Divide this figure by 4.5 for Imperial gallons or by 3.8 for US gallons. Deduct 10% from the volume to allow for any gravel, tank decorations, etc.

3 Turn off activated carbon filters during treatment.

4 Do not overcrowd fish during treatment and ensure adequate aeration.

5 Always try out a remedy on one or two specimens before treating a whole batch of delicate or expensive fish.

6 Excessive amounts of organic matter will reduce the effectiveness of most remedies.

7 Never mix remedies unless you know it is safe. Carrying out a 50-75% water change or using an activated carbon filter for 12-24 hours should remove most of the active ingredients after each treatment is finished.

8 Remember that correct care and prompt treatment are vital for healthy fish.

9 Before returning cured fishes to the pond, re-acclimatize them to the water quality of the pond by gradually replacing the water in their treatment tank with water from the pond. This will help to prevent undue stress that exposure to a sudden change of water conditions can cause, and will thus help reduce the risk of any re-infection.

Slimy skin
Fishes afflicted with this condition develop a thin grey film over the body. The parasites *Cyclochaeta* and *Costia* (shown at below left, right) cause the fish to produce excessive amounts of slime.

Dropsy
The scales protrude noticeably due to accumulated liquid in the body. The fluid from infected fish may infect others. To prevent this happening remove any sick fishes promptly.

Fish diseases
This fish is unlucky to have all these ailments at once! Use this illustration as a diagnostic aid to help you recognize common disease symptoms and to prevent your fishes from ever reaching this sorry state.

Tailrot/Finrot
These very obvious symptoms appear on fishes of poor health. Physical damage and unhygienic conditions in the aquarium or pond all encourage the harmful bacterial action.

White spot
Tiny white spots cover the fins and body. A common parasitic ailment that some aquarists believe lies dormant in every aquarium or pond ready to afflict weak fishes.

Skin flukes
The *Gyrodactylus* parasites burrow into the fish's skin and stay near the surface. Affected fishes lose colour and become feeble. Responds well to treatments.

Eye infections
Cloudy eyes (below) are often due to larval worms, cataract or bacterial infection. Protruding eyes (main drawing) usually suggests that other diseases are present as well.

Fungus
Fungus *(Saprolegnia)* attacks fishes already weakend by physical damage, parasites, or poor conditions. Also liable to affect fishes if they are transferred to widely differing pond or aquarium waters.

Gill flukes
The flatworm *(Dactylogyrus)* attaches itself to the gill membranes. Affected fishes have faster respiration and gaping gills.

Mouth 'fungus'
This is caused by a bacterial infection. It is important to catch this infection as soon as it appears. Use an anti-bacterial treatment.

Pond fish diseases and treatment

The following diseases and parasitic infestations that may affect pond fish are fairly straightforward to recognize and should respond to the recommended treatment if it is given correctly and promptly.

Anchor worm (*Lernaea sp.*)

Female anchor worms (the principal parasitic stage of the organism) resemble small twigs, about 20mm (0.8in) long, hanging onto the fishes' body. They occur most often on freshly introduced fish. In the spring, two egg sacs are visible at the end of the long thin body. The organism itself is not a worm but a tiny crustacean, which can be seen more clearly if the 'twig' is carefully pulled out with a pair of tweezers. By piercing the skin, anchor worms expose the fish to secondary infections, which normally create further health problems.

Treatment: Several proprietary treatments are available that can be added to the pond and will kill all the larval stages in the complex life

cycle of the anchor worm. The most widely available treatments contain the organophosphorus compound dimethyltrichlorohydroxyethyl phosphonate. (This is available under various trade names, including Dipterex, Dylox and Masoten.) Use such treatments strictly according to the directions. (Local regulations affect availability of drugs.)

It is possible to remove the adult parasites by hand using fine tweezers. (This involves anaesthetizing the fish in a suitable bowl or baby bath. Follow drug instructions implicitly. If you are unsure, seek veterinary help.) Treat the wound with mercurochrome or providone-iodine applied with a soft camel-hair brush or cotton bud. Keep the fish in a fungicidal and bacterial bath until you are sure that recovery is complete.

Carp pox

This viral disease seems to occur in crowded conditions. It manifests itself as opalescent, greasy-looking white spots that can become quite large. When the infection is at an advanced stage, they merge and take on a reddish grey appearance.

Treatment: If you clean out and thoroughly disinfect the filter, the problem should disappear after

Below: *An anchor worm is clearly visible on this Koi. As the common name suggests, the adult stage of this crustacean parasite literally 'anchors' itself in the skin.*

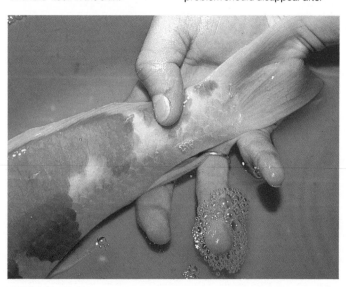

Above: *These greasy blobs are typical of the viral disease carp pox, or skin papilloma. No treatment is available, but affected fishes usually recover in clean conditions.*

eight to twelve weeks. There is no known treatment as such, but the disease is not normally fatal, and will usually cure itself in time.

Cloudy eye

With this disease, one or both eyes may become clouded over and opaque. A fish will lose its appetite and become listless. This is a non-specific infection and may be caused by parasitic as well as bacterial infections.

Treatment: Make sure that the conditions are as clean and healthy as possible and add a little salt to the water – at the rate of 3gm per litre (0.5oz per gallon). If a parasite, such as *Oodinium* (velvet disease), is detected then treat it with an appropriate antiparasitic remedy. Otherwise use an antibacterial.

Columnaris

(*Flexibacter columnaris*)
This is a virulent bacterial disease, misleadingly referred to as 'mouth fungus' because of the greyish white film it produces. It usually attacks the head region, which can result in the mouthparts and adjacent areas being eaten away, but it can attack any part of the body. It is highly contagious.

Treatment: Remove all affected fish from the pool at once. Place them in a weak salt solution and keep the water very clean by filtration. Sterilize all nets and utensils after use. Products containing phenoxyethanol, nifurpirinol, nitrofurazone and benzalkonium chloride are some recommended treatments. Follow manufacturer's instructions closely.

Below: *This greyish white film is caused by the bacterial infection* Columnaris. *Typically found on the head region, it may also affect other parts of the fish, as shown here.*

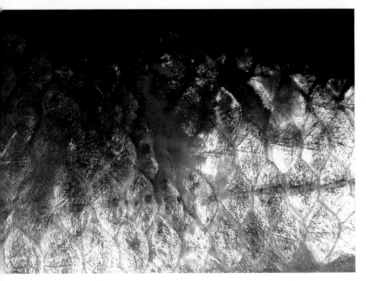

Dropsy (*Ascites*)

Dropsy is often known as 'pine-cone disease' because one of the symptoms is that the scales stand out from the body. The chief characteristic, however, is a swollen abdomen. Affected fishes also swim and breathe with difficulty. Eventually the eyes and head also become swollen. Various bacteria are responsible for this condition, which is normally fatal. However, a

Above: *The swollen abdomen and protruding scales are clear signs of dropsy, a bacterial infection that may prove fatal if not treated.*

cure may be attempted and this is sometimes effective.

Treatment: Antibacterial treatment and salt baths are worth trying. Using oxolinic acid to make medicated food may also help.

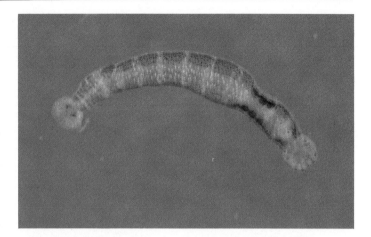

Finrot and tailrot (*Aeromonas hydrophila* and other species)
This condition generally occurs when the fish are living in unsatisfactory conditions. The bacteria are normally present on the fish, and only attack as a result of damage or stress caused during travelling and handling. The first symptom is the appearance of opaque patches on the fins, but the infection quickly develops to an acute stage when the fins rot away, leaving bloody fin rays. Ultimately, the entire fin is destroyed and the body itself is attacked. At this stage, the fish is doomed to die. As with other diseases, the affected fish is vulnerable to attack by secondary fungal, viral or bacterial infections.

Treatment: Consult your veterinarian, who may anaesthetize the fish and cut away the infected portions of the fins. Providing the disease is caught early enough, phenoxyethanol, nifurpirinol, nitrofurazone, benzalkonium chloride and chloramine are effective. Follow the manufacturer's instructions when using these.

Left: *Koi with signs of finrot. Unchecked, the infection (caused by various bacteria) eventually causes the fins to disintegrate and may then spread onto the body. Use proprietary remedies as directed and maintain clean conditions in the pond.*

Above: *A fish leech,* Piscicola geometra, *in a 'relaxed' position. When 'extended', it may reach up to 3cm (1.2in) in length. Leeches in general do not usually pose a serious health problem in Koi ponds, although they can pass on infections and cause body damage that may become infected.*

Fish leech (*Piscicola geometra*)
There are dozens of species of freshwater leeches, but they seldom cause any problem to the fish. However, occasionally a pond may become infested with the dangerous types. Fish leeches are worm-like, but flattened, and they crawl and swim in a series of looping motions. Infected fish will rub themselves vigorously against hard objects. Close inspection may reveal the presence of leeches, which may be up to 3cm (1.2in) long, clinging to the body. They are normally brown or greyish in colour.

Treatment: Remove the fish from the pool and place it in a three percent salt solution for a short time. The leeches will either drop off or may be removed gently by hand. (After about ten minutes the fish will become unconscious and should be removed at once.) Do not attempt to remove the leeches without first using the salt, or the mouth parts may be left in the skin, giving rise to nasty infections. Clearing the pool is more difficult.

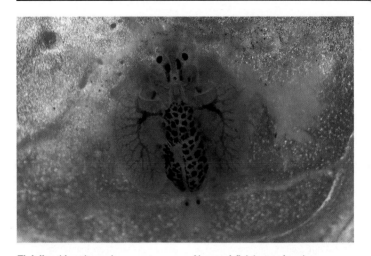

Fish lice (*Argulus* sp.)

The fish louse is a common parasite on newly imported Koi. It is a parasitic crustacean 8-12mm (0.3-0.5in) in diameter, and is easily recognizable with the naked eye. It attaches itself to the fish by its paired suckers and draws blood from the fish through a needle-like proboscis, causing inflammation and anaemia.

Treatment: Treat the pond water with a course of a proprietary preparation containing dimethyltricholorohydroxyethyl phosphonate, such as Dipterex, Dylox or Masoten. Treating individual fish involves using a short-term bath (see table) and dabbing mercurochrome or povidone-iodine on the wounds.

Above: *A fish louse,* Argulus foliaceus, *clinging to the skin. The suckers, the parasite's means of attachment, look like eyes.*

Fungus (Principally *Saprolegnia*)

This disease first appears in small patches resembling cotton wool. They often occur on the site of an injury. Although normally white, the presence of unicellular algae will often give the fungal growth a greenish appearance. Once it takes a hold, it can quickly cover the entire body. The fungal filaments are anchored in the skin and absorb nutrients from the fishes' body.

Below: *A Koi with fungal growths attached to the skin. Their green appearance is caused by the accumulation of green algal cells.*

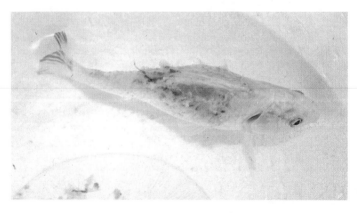

Treatment: Use a mixture of malachite green and common salt, or malachite green and formalin (3.3gm malachite green solid/1 litre formalin).

Gill flukes
(*Dactylogyrus* and other species)
Koi heavily infested with gill flukes show an increased respiratory rate and gaping gills. The fish will 'mouth' at the surface. The organisms responsible are very small worm-like creatures known as monogenetic trematodes. (The term 'monogenetic' means that their parasitic life cycle occurs entirely in one host.) The parasites, each up to 1mm (0.04in) long, attach to the gills by hooks and can soon devastate the gill filaments if left untreated.

Treatment: Use one of the many good proprietary antiparasitic treatments available as directed.

Pop-eye (*Exophthalmus*)
With this disease, one or both eyes begin to protrude progressively from the socket. In the later stages, the eye may be expelled and blindness occurs. This condition can be caused by many organisms.

Treatment: A combination of antiparasitic and antibacterial treatments may be effective.

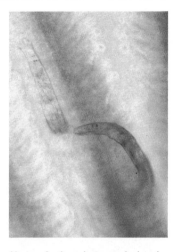

Above: *A microphotograph showing two gill flukes* (Dactylogyrus *sp.*) *attached to the gill filaments. A heavy infestation causes gaping gills and may lead to permanent damage if left untreated. Gill flukes are a particular hazard for baby fishes and for adults in a weakened condition. Treatment is effective.*

Below: *Protruding eyes, a condition known as 'pop-eye', may result from a variety of causes. These include certain parasites invading the eye (larval trematodes responsible for worm cataracts), bacterial infections and dropsy.*

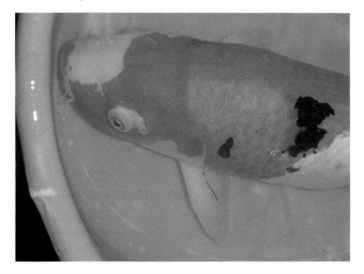

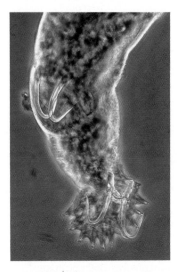

To treat the pond water use a mixture of malachite green and formalin following the guidelines in the table on pages 150-151.

Swimbladder trouble
This is one of the most common problems with the Carp family. Affected fish are unable to maintain their balance and may assume unnatural positions in the water. They may swim head down, upside down, or may even be unable to move off the bottom of the pool. Sometimes the problem has its origins in bacterial infection, but in carp it may be due to an organic malfunction of the swimbladder.

Treatment: There is no definite cure for this condition. However, placing the fish in shallower, warmer water to which a small dose of salt is added, can sometimes result in a cure, although the fish may suffer permanent after-effects.

Above: *A microphotograph of a skin fluke,* Gyrodactylus *sp. The hooks are clearly visible at the base, as are those of a juvenile inside the adult.*

Skin flukes (*Gyrodactylus*)
These trematode parasitic worms are closely related to gill flukes (*Dactylogyrus* sp.). Affected fish will rub themselves against hard objects, often with a skimming motion, in their efforts to relieve the irritation caused by the flukes embedded in the skin. Each fluke may be up to 0.8mm (0.03in) long. The skin of affected fishes loses its sparkle and appears whitish or inflamed.

Treatment: Use a proprietary antiparasitic remedy as instructed by the manufacturer.

Sliminess of the skin (Unicellular parasites such as *Costia, Chilodonella, Trichodina* sp.) These parasites cause the skin to take on a greyish appearance as the fish produces excess mucus in reaction to their presence. Affected fishes will rub against hard objects or against the bottom of the pond in their irritation.

Treatment: Broad-spectrum antiparasitic chemicals are effective against these unicellular parasites.

Tapeworms
These internal parasites often have complex life cycles. *Bothriocephalus acheilognathi* is a species that has been found in some batches of imported fish. Common in China and Japan, it has now spread to many sites in Europe. The adult stage in Koi can cause blockage, intestinal perforation and peritonitis. Some tapeworms, such as *Ligula intestinalis*, infest Koi only as an intermediate host in the cycle.

Treatment: Consult a veterinarian who may use praziquantel or a similar drug to treat infested fish.

Ulcer disease
Infection is due to several species of bacteria, including the *Aeromonas* and *Pseudomonas* species. It has led to great losses in the commercial world during the last ten years. Shallow open sores appear on the body, the base of the fins and sometimes the anus. Although the lesions are superficial, they increase rapidly, leading to chronic septicaemia (blood poisoning), dropsy and death. A great deal of research has been carried out on

Above: *Evidence of 'hole disease', which has similar symptoms to ulcer disease. Both of these bacterial infections cause lesions in the body which, if left untreated, can lead to the death of the fish.*

this disease but with little success. It is highly contagious, and sick fish should be isolated at once. Fish can be carriers without showing overt symptoms of the disease.

Below: *A close-up view of the distinctive symptoms of white spot disease, or ich, on a fin.*

Treatment: Antibiotics or oxolinic acid added to the food seem to be the most effective cure. Salt is useful as a supportive treatment.

White spot disease, or ich
(*Ichthyophthirius*)
This well-known condition (known in Japan as 'Hakuten'), is caused by a unicellular parasite that infests fish at the free-swimming stage of its life cycle. The parasites burrow into the skin and live just beneath the outer skin layer, causing the body and fins to become covered in small white spots about 1mm (0.04in) in diameter. If left untreated, secondary infections, both bacterial and fungal, become established and eventually kill the fish. Untreated fish can die in a few days.

Treatment: Use a white spot proprietary remedy, malachite green, or malachite green and formalin as indicated on pages 150-151. The treatment works more quickly if the water temperature is raised to at least 26°C (79°F). Increase the aeration to compensate for the lower oxygen levels in warmer water.

Guidelines for using chemicals

Chemical	Concentration mg/litre (ppm)	Dosage range per 100 litres
Benzalkonium chloride	Bath: 1-4	0.2-0.8ml
Chloramine T	Bath: 2.2 Pool: 0.5	0.2gm 0.05gm
Dimethyltrichloro-hydroxyethyl-phosphonate	Bath: 22 Pool: 0.3	2.2gm 0.03gm
Formalin (A solution containing approx. 37% formaldehyde)	Bath: 24 Pool: 13.5	2.4ml 1.3ml
Formalin and malachite green mixture	Pool: Formalin 15 and malachite green 0.05	1.5ml of mixture
Levamisole	Bath: 10	1gm
Malachite green	Bath: 0.4 (*1) Pool: 0.2 (*1)	2ml 1ml
Methylene blue	Bath: 2(*2)	8ml
MS 222 Anaesthetic	Bath: 25-100	2.5-10gm
Ni furpirinol	Bath: 1-4 Pool: 0.25	0.1-0.4gm 0.025gm
Nitrofurazone	Bath: 1-3	0.1-0.3gm
Oxolinic acid	5gm per kg of treated food	Give treated food at rate of 1% of fish body weight per day
Oxytetracycline	Bath: 13-120 In food: 50mg per kg of fish	1.3-12gm
Para-chloro-phenoxyethanol	Bath: 20	1.8ml
Phenoxyethanol	Bath: 100 Food: Soak in 1% solution (10gm/litre)	9.1ml
Sodium chloride (Common salt)	Bath: 30,000 (3%)	3kg
	Bath/Pool: 10,000(1%)	1kg
	Pool: 3,000(0.3%)	300gm

(*1) Parts per million (ppm) based on solid. Dosages based on 2% solution in water.
(*2) ppm based on solid. Dosages based on 2.5% solution in water. To convert dosages for 100 Imperial gallons and 100 US gallons, multiply figures in 'Dosage range' column by

Treatment time	Other details	Effective against
60 mins	Dosage based on liquid formulation containing 50% active ingredient	Columnaris, finrot, tail-rot and other external bacterial diseases
60 mins Continuous until cured. Repeat after 3 days	Available as powder. Maximum of 3 consecutive treatments	Slime disease, white spot, skin flukes, myxobacterial gill disease, external bacterial diseases
60 mins Continuous until cured. In hard water repeat after 7 days	Maximum 3 consecutive treatments. Products: Dipterex, Dylox, Masoten, Neguvon, Trichlorphon	Fish lice, anchor worms and other parasites, such as skin and gill flukes
30 mins Continuous until cured. Repeat after 7 days	Rarely used alone. Normally used with malachite green, see below. Aerate water	Combined with malachite green: fungus, slime disease, white spot, skin and gill flukes
Continuous until cured	Use 3.3gm of malachite green solid in one litre of formalin	Fungus, slime disease, white spot, and skin and gill flukes
12-24 hours		Intestinal worms
30 mins Continuous until cured. Repeat after 7 days	Use with formalin or sodium chloride	Fungus, slime disease, white spot, other parasites, such as skin flukes
Continuous until cured	Do not use with biological filters; it will disrupt their action	Traditional treatment for fungus, protozoan parasites. Commercial remedies better
1-3 mins, depending on pH, temperature, size and condition of fish	Requires care. Consult veterinarian or other skilled person	
60 mins Continuous until cured	If difficult to obtain, consider using para-chloro-phenoxyethanol	Columnaris, finrot, tailrot, plus other bacterial and fungal diseases
60 mins	If difficult to obtain, consider using para-chloro-phenoxyethanol	Columnaris, finrot, tailrot, plus other bacterial and fungal diseases
Use for 10 days	Available ready mixed with food; take advice from veterinarian	Dropsy, ulcer disease, plus other bacterial diseases
Continuous until cured Use for 7 days	Antibiotic. Use lower concentration unless hard water reduces effect	Bacterial diseases
Continuous until cured	Take care to dissolve and disperse throughly	Fungus, finrot, tailrot, and other bacterial diseases
Continuous until cured Use for 7 days	Supplied as oily liquid Take care to dissolve and disperse thoroughly	Fungus, columnaris, finrot, tailrot. Use soaked food against nematode worms
Up to 10 mins	Remove fish immediately if it shows distress	Cloudy eye and parasites. (Increases mucus flow)
1-2 weeks	Use with malachite green or phenoxyethanol	Supportive for various diseases and wounds/ulcers
Continuous until cured		General protection, e.g. against nitrite toxicity*

4.55 and 3.79 respectively. Internationally accepted chemical names used where possible. Local regulations affect availability of drugs. Seek veterinary advice.

Breeding fish

In nature and in the pond, the onset of spring followed by the warmer summer provides the stimulus for spawning. At the same time, the amount of live natural foods also increases, and this brings the adult fishes into the peak of condition. After spawning occurs, there is still plenty of time for the fry to grow and feed before the cold months arrive again, and they can build up their reserves to overwinter successfully.

Of course, with fish in the outdoor pond, the fishkeeper has little control over spontaneous spawnings (beginners often not realizing it is even occurring) and therefore no control over which fishes spawn together. Goldfish, being a single species, will readily interbreed no matter what colour pattern or finnage they exhibit as individuals. This means that quality is soon lost unless 'selected partners' only are allowed to breed, and this is best done in a specially set-up aquarium.

Spawning is likely to occur once water temperatures have risen in late spring and remain high. The first sign you are likely to see of spawning activity will be some fishes chasing others into the oxygenating plants, especially in shallow areas where the water is even warmer. At the end of such frenzied activity, close examination

Left: *A male Stickleback energetically fans the eggs that have been laid in a tunnel nest built from plant fragments. He guards them until they hatch.*

Above: *The tubercles on the gill plates and pectoral fins of this Goldfish show that it is in a breeding condition, not diseased as might be supposed.*

of the plants will reveal lots of tiny eggs among the leaves. Remove the whole bunch of egg-laden plants to a separate aquarium (or smaller, fish-less pond) for hatching to occur. If left in the main pond, the fry may be eaten by other fish and predatory waterborne insect larvae. To maximize certainty of raising quality fish, and where surviving numbers are important, aquarium spawning is recommended.

Sexing goldfish
During the breeding season, the body of the mature female will take on a full rounded appearance, especially when viewed from above. The mature male develops pale 'tubercles' – small bumps or pimples – on his head, gill covers and pectoral fins. This makes the male rough to the touch and he will use these tubercles to rub against the female during courtship.

The sex of the fish can be confirmed by their behaviour at spawning time, when the male will actively chase the female for several days before spawning begins. Immature fish, or fish outside their breeding season, can be difficult to sex reliably.

Choosing the parent fish
It is vital that you choose the potential parent fish – or 'brood stock' – with care, since these fish will pass on their best – and worst – characteristics to their offspring. You will need one, or perhaps, two males to each female and you should, of course, avoid interbreeding different varieties. If necessary, you can prevent indiscriminate spawning by putting the males and females in separate tanks, or by keeping them on opposite sides of a tank divider.

Obviously, the brood stock must be healthy. They should show good finnage and coloration and should swim normally. Avoid fish with deformities, those which are noticeably slow growing, and any that were slow to change colour when juveniles. Willingness to feed is a good sign of a healthy fish.

Preparations for spawning
Correct nourishment is vital if your goldfish are to breed successfully. This means that in the few weeks before spawning the fish need a balanced and varied diet that includes both good-quality prepared food and live food, such as earthworms and bloodworms.

This will bring the fish into ripe spawning conditions and also make up any losses of 'live food' advantages the fish might have otherwise received in the outdoor pond. Resist the temptation to overfeed, which may result in an accumulation of uneaten food.

Aquarium breeding
The spawning tank should be fairly roomy, 100 litres (22 gallons) or so, and furnished with clumps of bushy egg-catching plants or artificial spawning mops made of nylon wool strands tied in a bundle. The male will drive the female into these clumps, and eggs will be trapped in them and hidden from the adult fishes, who would otherwise probably eat them. The adult fishes can be removed after spawning and the eggs left in the mops to hatch; or the mops can be removed to another convenient tank and the eggs hatched there. Eggs hatch in about four days at 21°C (70°F).

Below: *Ranchu spawning among Hornwort* (Ceratophyllum).

Care of the fry
When the fry hatch, they will not need food immediately, as they take a little while to absorb the yolk sac; but they will need food as soon as they have become free-swimming. Any addition of food to the water before this time is unnecessary. First foods can be cultivated infusoria cultures (microscopic single-celled animals, such as *Paramecium*) or one of the proprietary brands of liquid or powdered fry foods; details on culturing larger live foods follow.

From here on, it is a matter of keeping fry well fed and well spread out (in extra tanks) if there is a very large number of them. They should be culled from time to time, discarding the deformed or tiny ones (or those that obviously will not conform to accepted show standards). Don't be tempted to save too many youngsters and, above all, don't return excessive numbers back to the pond; the number of young fish resulting from spontaneous spawnings in the pond is usually kept down by predation.

FRY FOODS

Here, we look at how to culture live foods suitable for very young fry. Further guidance on feeding is given on pages 40-45.

Infusorians

Infusorians are tiny single-celled animals that occur in almost all water. They are an ideal first food for very tiny goldfish fry, and they can be cultured quite easily in containers such as large glass jars. To ensure a continuous supply, you will need to start a new culture every 3-4 days.

Three-quarters fill a jar with cooled boiled tapwater. Drop in three or four bruised lettuce leaves or a banana skin. You can even pour some boiling water over a little hay, in order to break up the cells, and add the hay to the jar. Place the jar, with the lid off, in a warm, moderately well-lit place. Over the next few days, the culture should go cloudy and begin to smell slightly. It will start to clear as the infusorians develop. Once the culture is clear and sweet-smelling, you can pour or siphon it into the fry tank, a little at a time.

Obviously, it is important to have the infusorians ready as the fry 'come on to feed', and to maintain a satisfactory supply until the fry accept other foods.

Brineshrimp

There can be few hobbyists breeding fish who have not heard of the brineshrimp (*Artemia salina*). This tiny saltwater crustacean is frequently used as a food for recently hatched fish fry. It is still the main standby for carp farmers when rearing very young fry. Brineshrimp eggs are available from most pet shops and aquarium stores. However, it is sometimes a false economy to buy them in bulk because, if stored in unsatisfactory conditions, the hatchability of the eggs will decrease markedly with time. For best results, store the eggs in a cool dry place.

Culturing brineshrimp is relatively easy. You can buy a brineshrimp hatchery from a pet shop, but you can also achieve good results using several clean glass bottles.

Set up the 'bottle hatchery' in a warm room. The temperature should be at least 15°C (59°F), although the eggs will hatch more quickly – within 24-48 hours – at 20-25°C (68-77°F).

Pour about 400ml (approximately three-quarters of a pint) of cooled boiled water into a bottle. Add 8-12gm (about 2-3 level teaspoons) of cooking salt. (You may obtain better results using marine salts.) Aerate the salt water vigorously, then leave it to reach room temperature. Add about a quarter of a teaspoon (or less) of brineshrimp eggs. It is a good idea to put a cotton wool bung in the neck of the bottle. Remember that for the eggs to hatch successfully, they must be kept in warm, saline and well-aerated water.

One or two days after starting the first culture, set up a second bottle in the same way, followed by a third after another couple of days. The eggs will hatch after 24-48 hours in a warm room and, by starting several cultures in succession, you will ensure the availability of newly hatched brineshrimp for a week or so. By this time, the fry should accept finely powdered dried foods.

To separate the newly hatched brineshrimp from the egg shells and unhatched eggs, turn off the aeration for a few minutes. The living brineshrimp will collect in a layer about 2.5-5cm (1-2in) from the bottom of the bottle and can be siphoned out using a piece of airline. Top up the bottle with dechlorinated saline water, and turn the aeration back on. Each culture should last for 2-3 days.

Breeding Koi

Males should be at least two years old and females should be over three years of age. The stock does not need to be of show quality in order to produce a proportion of well-coloured youngsters. In fact, show-quality Koi and prize winners are seldom used for breeding since it is a very hectic business which may lead to loss of scales and a deterioration in condition.

Male Koi are slender, with a comparatively large head and pectoral fins. When in breeding condition, tubercles (white dots) appear on the pectoral fins and on the gill plates. Female Koi are fatter and can appear slightly lop-sided since the spawn often hangs more heavily on one side of the body than the other. It is usual to mate one female to two or three males, as this ensures a higher fertilization rate.

Koi lay between 100,000 and 750,000 eggs, depending on the size and condition of the female. The eggs are a transparent greenish colour and only 0.33mm (approximately 0.1in) in diameter. They are sticky and adhere to any

Below: Koi spawning among ropes and conifer branches. The sticky greenish eggs readily adhere to the strands of the spawning medium.

finely divided material. Spawning mats may be synthetic, such as nylon brushes, or they can be natural materials, such as water plants and conifer branches. Many breeders use the Water Hyacinth (*Eichhornia crassipes*), which has highly suitable long trailing roots.

While fish can spawn in the pool in which they live, it is more usual to prepare a special breeding pool. Ideally this pool should be about 2.4x1.8m (8x6ft) and 45cm (18in) deep, with the spawning medium placed at one end. When you see that your breeders are ready to spawn, net them carefully and place them in the breeding pool. Do not feed them during this period. Courtship normally occurs during the morning hours, with the female being continually chased by the males as they drive her towards the

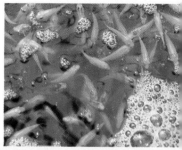

spawning ground. As soon as spawning has finished, remove the breeders quickly as they will attempt to eat the eggs.

Remove the eggs (still attached to the spawning medium) and place them in a solution of malachite green of a concentration 1:300,000. Leave them for fifteen minutes to disinfect them and then put them back in the breeding pond to hatch. At 21-24°C (70-75°F), they will hatch in four to seven days. Lower or higher temperatures will slow down or speed up the hatching rate respectively. Two or three days after hatching, the fry will become free swimming.

Newly hatched brineshrimp or sifted *Daphnia* are the best first foods. Keep them on these foods for about a month before weaning them on to suitable dried foods.

Left: *A mass of Koi fry in a breeding pond. Overcrowding can lead to cannibalism and spread of disease.*

Below: *Selected young Koi being groomed for possible international stardom on a Japanese Koi farm.*

Culling

Young Koi should be separated by colour at the age of one month. This is the start of the process of selecting the best individuals for subsequent rearing. Do not attempt to rear all the Koi: select only those that you can comfortably house and discard the unwanted individuals. (The most humane way of killing fish is to chill them with ice cubes.) Keep only 10-20 percent of the fish. Overcrowded fry become cannibalistic and are prone to disease, which can spread quickly.

Showa may be selectively culled after only 14 days. Wait 50 days for Ogon, and 60 days for Kohaku and Taisho Sanke. Weed out all plain white fish and any with deformities. Do not forget that culling is carried out for pattern and quality, and only experience can guide you in this extremely important selection process.

As the fish grow up, further culling is necessary until, by the time they reach 7.5cm (3in) in length, hopefully you will have selected some interesting possibilities in terms of colour and pattern.

Goldfish

When fish are to be chosen for the pond various factors have to be taken into account. The pond will be affected by all the seasonal changes, often with extremes of temperature. The fish should be colourful enough to be seen easily, they should not grow too big too quickly, and should certainly not be likely to eat any of the water plants. Happily, there is one species of fish that fits the bill to perfection – even if you are not a fishkeeper you will know it.

Although many types of fish may be kept in ponds, the Goldfish remains the most popular species, and is probably everyone's first choice when stock for the pond is considered. Its general hardiness and wide temperature adaptability both ensure that it will be suitable for the broad range of conditions it is likely to meet in ponds around the world; add to these two qualities its readiness to breed, bright colours, ready appetite and low purchase cost, and you have an ideal supply of very suitable pond fish. Goldfish are long-lived – 20 years is not uncommon – and they adapt themselves to the size

of their environment very well, not outgrowing an indoor aquarium, yet reaching adequate proportions in a reasonable-sized pond.

Despite being a single species, thanks to the perseverance of fishkeepers down the centuries, the Goldfish has been developed into many diverse, yet firmly established, strains. The attraction of these strains may be less obvious in some of the more exotic varieties (whose physical forms are much removed from that of the original fish) and many of these are not physically suited for pond life; in addition, the black coloration of the Moor, for instance, would make it much less visible in an outdoor pond. However, provided the pondkeeper limits the selection of Goldfish to a few hardy varieties (still with many varying colour strains, differing scale patterns and finnage forms to choose from), these will more than repay the effort involved in maintaining their living conditions, with vibrant colours, flowing fins, healthy activity and trouble-free increase in stock. Who could ask for a better pond fish?

History and origins

The Goldfish (*Carassius auratus*) is without doubt the most popular pet fish in the world, and its association with the human race goes back 1600 years. It is the domesticated form of a small wild carp found in still and slow-flowing waters in Southern China, which resembles the European Crucian Carp (*Carassius carassius*).

During the Chin Dynasty (265-420 AD), Chinese fish breeders noticed that some of the rather drab green-brown local carp occasionally produced individual offspring with attractive red scales. Eventually, after patiently experimenting with breeding, they produced fish with more and more attractive coloration. By 1200-1300, silver, black, gold and even mottled fish were available, and these became quite popular as pets. By the late 1500s, variations in fin shape, such as fantails and veiltails, began to appear. These were followed by different patterns and body forms – and even new

History of the goldfish

China
Coloured wild fish 400AD.
Colour forms as pets by 1200.
Variations from 1600.

Japan
Introduced in 1500.
Breeding established by 1700.

Europe
Widespread during the 1700s.

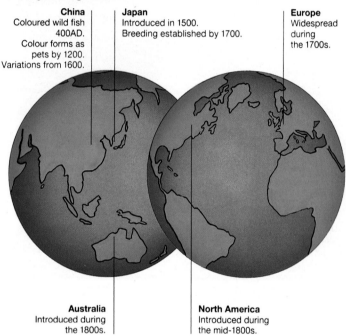

Australia
Introduced during the 1800s.

North America
Introduced during the mid-1800s.

China Coloured wild fish were observed around 400 AD. Various colour forms became available and were common as pets by 1200. Variations in body and fin shape appeared from about 1600.
Japan Goldfish were introduced from China around 1500. Breeding was established by about 1700 and was followed by the development of some fancy forms.
Far East Goldfish were widespread by 1700.

British Isles Goldfish were introduced around 1700.
Continental Europe Goldfish become widespread during the 1700s.
Russia Goldfish were introduced by the late 1700s.
North America Goldfish were probably introduced during the mid-1800s.
Australia and New Zealand Goldfish were introduced during the 1800s.

NATURAL SELECTION AND FISH BREEDING

Every species of animal continually produces 'mutations' among its offspring. These mutations should not be regarded as 'monsters', but rather as individuals often only showing slight physical or physiological differences from their parents and siblings.

Most frequently, these slightly different offspring are less well adapted for survival in their natural environment and they usually die before reaching maturity. Occasionally, however, the mutations may actually be better suited for survival, and therefore will be more likely to breed. They may produce offspring with similar advantageous characteristics.

This whole process is known as 'natural selection'. It results in gradual changes occurring in successive generations. As a result, the animals may become better adapted for life in their particular, and perhaps changing, environment.

In the case of the Goldfish, artificial selection by fish breeders, rather than natural selection by nature, has been the motive force for change. The Chinese fishkeepers of 1600 years ago noticed naturally occurring mutations among their native carp, and used these for selective breeding. Over many hundreds of years, selective breeding by fish breeders across the world has produced the many and varied types of fancy goldfish that we see today. All these varieties belong, of course, to one species (*Carassius auratus*) and they will all interbreed. In fact, the Goldfish will also interbreed with the closely related Crucian Carp.

It is interesting that when fancy goldfish are released into the wild, there is a gradual reversion to the green-brown wild form over a number of generations. The processes of natural selection and predation by other fish and birds quickly removes the more fancy and brightly coloured fish from the population. It is almost as if 1600 years of artificial selection can be undone in just a few years of natural selection.

eye shapes – by the 1600s. From this time onwards, further variations continued to appear in China and the interest in goldfish began to spread to other countries around the world.

Goldfish were taken to Japan, the home of the Koi carp (*Cyprinus carpio*), from China in around 1500, but it took another 200 years or so until goldfish breeding became established. Thereafter, Japanese fish breeders exerted their influence on this very variable fish, producing forms such as the lionhead and transparently scaled ('scaleless') variations such as the calico or shubunkin.

By the 1700s, goldfish had been introduced into many countries in the Far East. The opening up of trade and exploration routes around the world, together with the hardy nature of the goldfish and its ability to withstand long arduous journeys, no doubt aided the further spread of this fish around the world.

The goldfish first appeared in the United Kingdom in about 1700, or perhaps a little earlier. Around this time, the British began goldfish breeding, and some of the progeny were sent to continental Europe. Throughout the 1700s, goldfish were introduced from a variety of sources into Western Europe, and they reached Russia by the late 1700s. Interestingly, many of the more fancy types of goldfish did not appear in Europe until the 1900s.

The goldfish is thought to have been introduced into North

America during the 1800s, although some people claim that this occurred as much as 200 years earlier. However, by the late 1800s a goldfish farm was established in Maryland, USA, and recently goldfish have been recorded in the wild in every state except Alaska. The 1800s also saw the introduction of goldfishes into Australia and New Zealand, and the species is now widespread in natural waters in both countries.

Fancy goldfish can now be found in most, if not all, countries of the world. In many areas they have escaped or have been introduced into natural waters, where they have established feral populations.

Today, many millions of goldfish are bred every year on fish farms in North America, Europe and the Far East for distribution to fishkeepers around the world. This fish is known as 'chin-yu' in China, 'kingyo' in Japan, 'poisson rouge' in France and 'goldfisch' in Germany. Its hardy nature and bright coloration will continue to endear it to future generations of fishkeepers, who will enjoy the challenge of maintaining and developing the more fancy and bizarre varieties.

GOLDFISH FACTS

Family:
Cyprinidae (Carp family)
Scientific name:
Carassius auratus
Origins:
Southern China
Distribution:
Now worldwide, in aquariums, ornamental pools and natural waters.
Distinguishing features:
The Common Carp and the Koi Carp (*Cyprinus carpio*) both have barbels around the mouth. The Goldfish has none. The Crucian Carp (*Carassius carassius*) has no barbels, but generally has a deeper body and a longer dorsal fin than the Goldfish.
Size and growth:
A length of 20-25cm (8-10in) at 5-6 years of age is normal for goldfishes. Specimens up to 30cm (12in) long and weighing 4.5kg (10lb) have been noted.
Lifespan:
A lifespan of 10-20 years is not uncommon. Records exist of goldfish living for more than 40 years.

Pigmentation in goldfishes

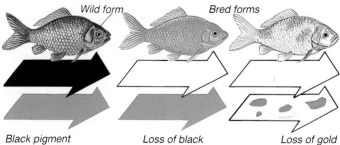

Wild form   Bred forms

Black pigment
overlays gold

Loss of black
reveals gold

Loss of gold
reveals white

*Above: Selective breeding has
removed the pigment cells which
give the wild goldfish (left) its drab
colour. Further loss of pigment
cells produce a white/ pink fish.
When cultivated goldfish are
released into natural waters, they
revert to more sombre colours.*

*Below: Continued selective
breeding has resulted in over a
hundred varieties of goldfish, some
showing evidence of the natural
variation inherent in the wild
goldfish population. This
spectacular fish is a Pearlscale
Veiltail Pompon Oranda.*

Goldfish varieties

Goldfish are available in over 100 different varieties. The features which distinguish them, such as coloration, body shape, finnage and the size and shape of the eyes, are the result of many years of selective breeding. Not everyone will find all the varieties attractive, but as there is such a wide choice, you should find at least one variety to suit you. This section describes a selection of the most popular ones.

It is best to avoid selecting the more exotic-looking varieties for a pond. Their flowing fins, together with other specially bred physical features, will be prone to damage (and resulting disease) in the outdoor pond, where water hygiene might not be as good as in a carefully maintained indoor aquarium. Their short stubby bodies (and in a few cases, lack of fins) also make them poor swimmers, so they may miss out at feeding times. They are somewhat delicate and, with the possible exception of the Fantail (see previous page), would not survive winter temperatures outside.

Above: **Common Goldfish**
A classic example of this robust and handsome beginner's fish.

Below: **Common Goldfish**
*A striking variation on a theme,
with black edges to the fins.*

Common Goldfish

The Common Goldfish is familiar to everyone. It has an evenly proportioned body and fins and may grow to about 23cm (9in), although it is usually much smaller if kept in a bowl or aquarium. The highest point of the shoulder should be above the pelvic fins, just before the start of the dorsal fin. The Common Goldfish has a shallow fork to its short tail fin.

A good specimen has metallic scales over the whole of the body. Yellow, red, orange, silver and even variegated fish are common.

The next two varieties may be seen as Japanese equivalents of the European Common Goldfish; despite their rather more exotic appearances, they are hardy.

The Wakin is the Common Goldfish of Japan. It has a double tail fin and may also occur with nacreous scales.

The Butterfly Tail Goldfish, or Jikin, is thought to have been developed from the Wakin and is rather similar to it. However, when viewed from behind, its double tail fin has a pronounced 'X' shape.

The Common Goldfish shown above provides a useful comparison for the London Shubunkin at above right and the Bristol Shubunkin shown at right, which has a significantly larger tail.

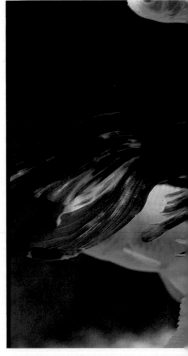

Shubunkin

Shubunkins, or Calico Goldfish, are beautiful and hardy fish. They have nacreous scales, i.e. pearly in appearance, and may reach 15cm (6in) or so in body length (23cm/9in in overall length).

The London Shubunkin has a body and fins similar to the Common Goldfish. It should have patches of red, yellow and black, along with dark speckles, on a bright blue background. This coloration and speckling usually extends over the fins of this very attractive fish.

Bristol Shubunkins are slim fish with well-developed fins. The tail fin, in particular, should be large and forked, with rounded ends. Its coloration is identical to the London Shubunkin.

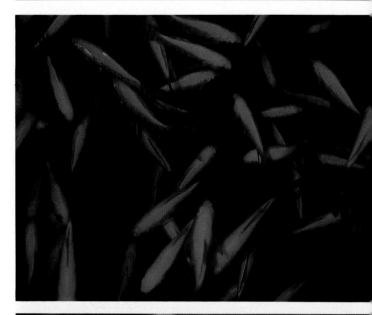

Comet
Also known as a Longtail, this is one of the fastest and most graceful of the Goldfish varieties. It is similar to the Shubunkin, but the longer caudal fin is deeply forked and at least three-quarters the length of the body. The other fins are flowing but very functional, making the fish very agile. The tail fin is single. The Comet is generally red, and shinier than the Shubunkin, but some are yellow; the preferred colour is a deep red-orange. Blue varieties are called Blue

Left: *A shoal of Comets. These are very fast and agile in the water, providing a continuous spectacle.*

Above: *The Sarasa Comets are noted for their bright red markings on a white background; they are hardy.*

Comets, and Sarasa Comets have strong red markings on a white background.

Comets are quite hardy and can be left to overwinter in the pond, although a pond heater is beneficial, and keeps the surface partly clear of

Above: *Comets are available in many colours, and the blue varieties are highly prized because of their rarity.*

ice. This fish is highly recommended for the garden pond, because of its brilliant colour and movement.

169

Koi

Nishikigoi, or Koi, are the national fish of Japan. 'Nishiki' is the Japanese word used to describe a highly coloured cloth. 'Goior Koi' is the Japanese name for carp. Together, therefore, 'Nishikigoi' means 'coloured carp'.

Iran is thought to be the ancestral home of the Common Carp (*Cyprinus carpio*), from which Koi were first developed. This wild carp, which is an excellent food, was carried to Japan, China and Western Europe by traders about a thousand years ago.

Koi were first bred in Japan in the 1820s, initially in the town of Ojiya, in the Niigata prefecture. Carp were used for food and were stored for eating during the winter. These brown fish produced occasional red and blue mutations, and selective breeding of these mutants resulted in the development of new varieties. By 1870, the Kohaku (red on white) variety was perfected. Many of the other currently recognized varieties were developed by the 1930s and new ones are being established all the time. In Europe, a mutation arose with only a few large glossy scales. This so-called Mirror Carp was sent from Germany to Japan, where it was crossbred to

produce varieties known as Doitsu-Goi, or German Carp.

Koi differ from Goldfish in their origins. Goldfish (*Carassius auratus*) share a common ancestry with the Crucian Carp (*Carassius carassius*) and were developed in China, where carp have been bred for at least 2000 years. They do not grow as large as Koi, and the two species can be clearly distinguished by the fact that Koi have two pairs of barbels on the upper lip, while Goldfish have none.

Koi-keeping is an immensely popular hobby in Japan, and Koi clubs hold many exhibitions and shows, with lavish prizes for the winners. The stakes can be high, with prize-winning fish changing hands for enormous sums of money.

Since the Second World War, Japan has exported many thousands of Koi to the West. Enthusiasts in North America and Western Europe have not only imported stock for sale, but have started fish farms in order to breed their own Koi. Koi are also bred in Israel and Singapore. So far, the fish produced have not matched the quality of those from Japan, but as knowledge of the techniques increases, no doubt the standard will improve.

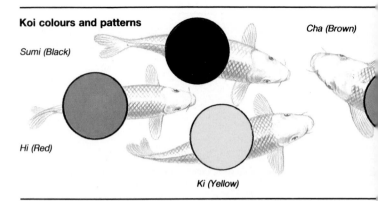

Koi colours and patterns

Sumi (Black)

Cha (Brown)

Hi (Red)

Ki (Yellow)

As mentioned in the first chapter, all Koi are developed from but a single species: the Common Carp (*Cyprinus carpio*). However, various mutations, such as the Mirror Carp of Europe, were crossbred with the original and it is from the type species, plus mutations, that all the current varieties are derived. These varieties have been given Japanese names which might prove confusing at first. However, these names are built up logically from 'components' that may refer to the period in which the variety was developed or to the colour, scale lustre, scale orientation, and finally to the pattern and distribution of colours.

Unlike other animals that breeders have developed along pedigree lines, Koi do not breed true. Having a pair of expensive show winners still means that from 40,000 fry from an adult pair, only about 20 might prove to be fish with acceptable standards of colour and pattern. Remember, too, that not all fish can be given a definite name and that many low grade fish will not fit into the recognized categories.

While the Goldfish has been deliberately bred for bizarre forms of fins, body and eyes, Koi breeders have concentrated on differences in the formation of scales, colour and patterning. However, this may change as Koi become 'international'; already, comet-tailed Koi are being produced. For simplicity, the Koi featured in this section of the book are presented according to the number of colours they have in their make-up. This

cuts across the traditional Japanese system of grouping Koi based on their genealogy, but it does form a useful way of introducing the range of Koi in a fairly straightforward manner. For reference, the Japanese groups are listed at the end of the section, on page 113.

First, we consider the scale types and then the colours in detail, with a selection shown in photographs.

Scale types
Four types of scale formation are recognized among the Koi varieties:

1 Scaled The most common fish with typical carp scales.

2 Doitsu A fish with scales along the dorsal and lateral lines only.

3 Leather A fish with no visible scales, except possibly very small scales along the dorsal line only.

4 Gin Rin A normally scaled fish which has a gold or silvery mirror like effect on the individual scales.

Colour types
This section is divided quite simply into single-colour, two-colour and three-colour fishes, with a mention of a multicolour type. The selection features the most important varieties available, plus a few of the more 'specialized' and rare ones. New ones are being developed all the time. Just to confuse matters, a single variety may be known by more than one name according to various authorities.

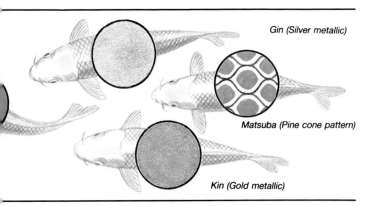

Gin (Silver metallic)

Matsuba (Pine cone pattern)

Kin (Gold metallic)

DESCRIPTIVE TERMS USED FOR KOI

The simplest terms used to name different varieties of Koi are the colours. Even here, though, confusion can arise. There are three terms for red, for example: 'Aka', 'Beni' and 'Hi'. The first two refer to an overall red colour, in conjunction with other descriptive terms, while the third is used to describe patches of red (on a white fish, for example). A similar situation arises with black, where 'Karasu' is used for a totally black fish and 'Sumi' for black patches. The list of common terms shown on this page will help you to understand how Koi names are built up, sometimes from a combination of several descriptive terms.

Aka	Red	**Muji**	Self-coloured
Akame	Eye with red iris		(literally 'nothing
Beni	Orange-red		else')
Bekko	Tortoiseshell	**Nezu**	Grey
Cha	Brown	**Ogon**	One-colour metallic
Doitsu	German type fish	**Orenji**	Orange
	with scales along	**Parrachina**	Very white metallic
	dorsal and lateral		(Platinum)
	lines only	**Rin**	Scale
Gin	Silver metallic	**Sanke, or**	Three-coloured fish,
Goi	Koi (short form of	**Sanshoku**	normally red, black
	Goior Koi)		and white
Hi	Red	**Shiro**	White
Inazuma	Lightning pattern	**Showa**	Era from 1926
Kabuto	Cap or helmet,		onwards
	referring to fish with	**Shusui**	Old variety from
	a head colour		1868-1926
	different from the	**Sui**	Water (rippling
	body		effect)
Karasu	Black (overall)	**Sumi**	Black (in the form of
Ki	Yellow		a patch)
Kin	Gold metallic	**Taisho**	Era 1912-1926
Kohaku	Red and white fish	**Tancho**	A bird (Tancho zura)
Kuchibeni	Red-lipped		with a red crest
Kujaku	Multicoloured	**Utsuri**	Reflecting
	(Peacock)	**Yamabuki**	Japonica bush with
Matsuba	Pine cone pattern		pale yellow flowers

173

Single-colour Koi

Above: *A mixed group of single-colour Koi, always popular* *throughout the world. The main photograph shows a superb gold*

Ogon (bottom left), a Parrachina (bottom right), a Kigoi (top left) and a Chagoi (top right). The inset features a Parrachina and a Benigoi.

Single-colour Koi may be some of the earliest varieties bred by direct mutation from the common carp or may be throwbacks as a result of crossbreeding multicoloured fish. They can be stunning in appearance.

WHITE

Shiromuji: Produced as a result of breeding Kohaku (Red on White), these fish are normally culled out or discarded when young due to their uninspiring appearance.

RED

Benigoi: Derived from the Kohaku, this fish shows only red coloration.

Below: **Kigoi**
A very attractive yellow Koi.

Hi Matsuba: Basically plain red but with the Matsuba pattern of darker scales giving a pine-cone effect.

YELLOW

Kigoi: These are produced from Asagi (Blue) or Kohaku (Red on White). The colour is a deep yellow in the best specimens, but is contaminated with white in poorer ones. Other varieties are Ki Matsuba, which is a prized fish with the Matsuba pine-cone effect picked out in blue on a yellow base-colour. Akame Kigoi is a yellow Koi with red eyes. Chagoi is a rare variety possessing a buff coloration. The Doitsu form sports a handsome pattern of large scales.

Below: **Chagoi**
A subtle shade of brownish-buff.

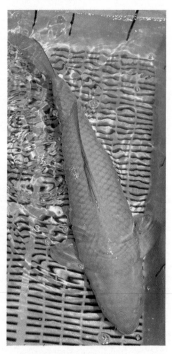

Right: **Ginrin Benigoi**
A rich red coloration combined with the 'mother of pearl' scales sparkling along the dorsal surface.

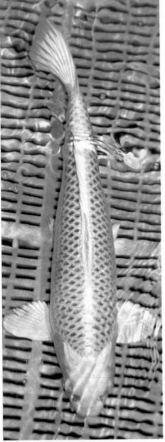

Above: **Kin Matsuba**
The Matsuba pattern in brown overlaid on a colour of sheer gold.

Above: **Ogon**
A stunning gold fish that is always one of the most popular varieties.

METALLIC

Ogon: Ogons are metallic Koi which are normally scaled, but which can be Doitsu or leather.

Kin Matsuba/Matsuba Ogon: This variety has a ground colour of gold with the Matsuba pattern of brown scales with gold edges along the back of the fish. This Matsuba type is derived from Asagi (Blue Koi).

Left: **Parrachina (Leather)**
A widely acclaimed variety with a smooth platinum-white sheen.

Parrachina/Shiro Ogon: This platinum variety is a result of a cross between Nezu-Ogon and an Akami Kigoi. It is probably one of the most popular varieties. (The word 'Parrachina' means 'very white metallic', i.e. suggesting a brilliant platinum effect.)

Gin Matsuba: This attractive platinum fish has the Matsuba (pine cone) pattern picked out in blue.

Orenji Ogon: An attractive fish that combines the metallic lustre of the Ogon with a basic orange colour. This form was first bred in 1956.

Above: **Orenji Ogon**
An impressive variety of a rich orange with a patina of gold.

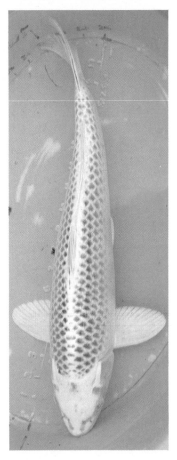

Above: **Gin Matsuba**
A subtle mix of platinum overlaid with the Matsuba pattern.

Two-colour Koi

Above: *A group shot featuring the following two-colour varieties of*

Koi: Inazuma Kohaku (large red and white fish); Shiro Bekko (mainly

white with black markings); Shiro
Utsuri (black with white markings);

Hi Utsuri (red and black); and Asagi
(light blue reticulated and red).

Two-colour Koi are designated by such terms as 'Black on Red' or 'Red on Black', which reflect the different parentages involved.

RED ON WHITE

Kohaku: Kohaku is the main pedigree line. It is a white Koi with red patterns. In most Koi contests in Japan the grand champion is a Kohaku. It was first named in 1899. The finest examples of Kohaku have a deep red coloration (Hi) in a sharp and distinct pattern. The white skin should be pure, with no stains or other blemishes. Unless the white is as pure as snow, the red pattern, no matter how good, will be reduced in value considerably. Sometimes black specks, known as 'Shimi', appear in the skin. The overall pattern should be balanced, with an interesting Hi marking that starts at the head and finishes near the tail.

The distance of white skin between the last Hi pattern and the tail is called 'Bongiri', which means 'tail closeout'.

There are many recognized types of Kohaku, including the folllowing:

Kuchibeni Kohaku: Kohaku with a red lipstick-like coloration of the lips. Not easily noticed from above.

Tancho Kohaku: Here, the body is basically white with a large circular red pattern, representing the sun, on the head. A very striking 'design'.

Nidan Kohaku: This name is given to Kohaku having a two-step pattern of red, i.e. two separate areas of colour on the white background.

Right: **Nidan Kohaku**
Two clear patches of red on white.

Below: **Tancho Kohaku**
A simple but very elegant pattern.

Left: **Sandan Kohaku**
A fine 'three-step' form of Kohaku.

Below: **Yondan Kohaku**
Four red patterns on a white ground.

Sandan Kohaku: Kohaku with a three-step pattern of red.

Yondan Kohaku: These fish have a four-step pattern of red.

Inazuma Kohaku: The word 'Inazuma' means lightning and is applied to Kohaku with a zig-zag pattern of red extending from head to tail. When the Inazuma patterns are large, the fish is called Omoyo; when small, the name Komoyo applies. An impressive variety.

Maruten Kohaku: Kohaku with an isolated Hi marking on the head (similar to that on the Tancho Kohaku – see photo on page 86) plus a Hi marking on the body.

Makibara Kohaku: In this type the red pattern extends around the stomach area.

Kanoko Kohaku: When the red pattern is dappled over the white body, not in a symmetrical way.

Goten-zakura Kohaku: When the spotted red pattern resembles clusters of grapes.

Kinzakura Kohaku: When the Gotenzakura scales are fringed with golden glints.

BLACK ON WHITE

Shiro Bekko: This type of Koi has a white body colour overlaid with blue-black markings (Sumi) that are mottled and extend into the fins but not into the head. Individuals with clear white fins and jet-black sumi markings are considered superior.

BLACK ON RED

Aka Bekko: This variety ideally has a deep red body with black mottling, which can extend into the fins.

Right: **Inazuma Kohaku**
A classic 'lightning' pattern of red.

Above: **Shiro Bekko**
White with black (Sumi) patches.

Left: **Maruten Kohaku**
One of several Kohaku varieties.

BLACK ON YELLOW

Ki Bekko: This is a striking yellow fish with black markings.

WHITE ON BLACK

Shiro Utsuri: This fish has white markings on a Sumi (black) background, giving a more marbled effect than in the Shiro Bekko. It was produced in 1925.

RED ON BLACK

Hi Utsuri: This Koi has a black background with red (Hi) markings. The more solid the markings the better, although many have black spots caused by unstable Sumi.

Right: **Shiro Utsuri**
A striking mix of black and white.

Below: **Hi Utsuri**
Look for a bold colour contrast in this red on black Koi variety.

Above: **Asagi**
Matsuba scales in light blue.

Right: **Shusui**
The 'straight' form of this hybrid.

190

YELLOW ON BLACK

Ki Utsuri: This rare Koi is the yellow counterpart of Shiro Utsuri, i.e. with yellow markings on a black body. The yellow generally extends into the fins. Crossed with Ogons, the Ki Utsuri produces a range of spectacular metallic types called Kin Ki Utsuri (shown on page 100).

RED AND BLUE

Asagi: In this Koi – developed from the Asagi Magoi – the body is generally light blue with a pine cone effect on the scalation. The cheeks, abdomen and the joints of the fins are red. The lower part of the abdomen is milky white. Several subvarieties of Asagi have been developed, varying in colour depth.

Shusui: This is an Asagi crossed with a Doitsu fish. The head should be light blue and the back a slightly darker blue. The tip of the nose, cheeks, abdomen and the joints of the fins are bright red. The large Doitsu scales should be in neat lines, especially the ones that run down the middle of the back. The latter must be dark blue. Several Shusui varieties are recognized, including the following two:

Hana Shusui: This type has red markings on the areas of blue skin between the abdomen and the lateral line and between the lateral line and the prominent line of scales along the dorsal region.

Hi Shusui: Here, the red of the abdomen spreads upwards and completely covers the dorsal region, with the large blue dorsal scales still in evidence.

Above: Hi Shusui
*In this form of Shusui the red
completely covers the upper parts.*

Right: Hana Shusui
*Shusui pattern but with red between
dorsal scales and abdomen.*

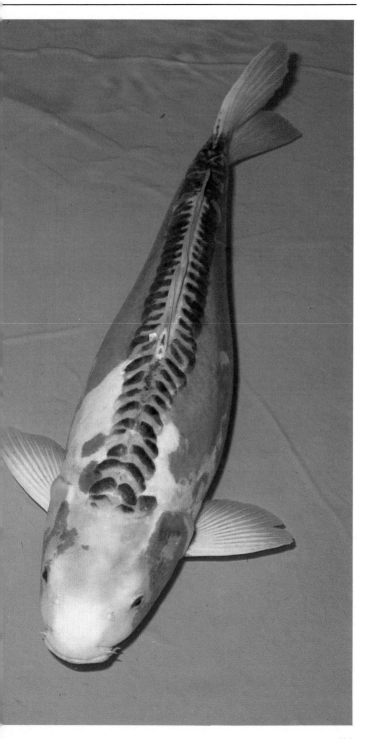

Above: Kujaku
*A handsome colour variety of Koi
that is basically a Yamabuki
Hariwake or an Orenji Hariwake with
a Matsuba (pine cone) overlay.*

Right: Hariwake
*The three types of Hariwake shown
here are: Yamabuki (top); Doitsu
(left); and Orenji (right). They are
among the most elegant of Koi types.*

METALLIC – VARIOUS COLOURS

Kinsui/Ginsui: Metallic Shusui. Those tinged in gold/red are called Kinsui and those with silver coloration are known as Ginsui.

Hariwake: This Koi has a predominately silver base colour with a gold pattern. There are many subvarieties of Hariwake with slight variations in coloration, including the following two:

Orenji Hariwake: A handsome fish in which orange-golden and platinum patterns predominate.

Yamabuki Hariwake: With patterns of bright golden yellow and platinum – an appealing combination.

Kujaku: A metallic Koi with Matsuba markings over a metallic yellow or orange and platinum base. (This and the following type are included with the Hariwake in the Hikarimoyo-mono Family.)

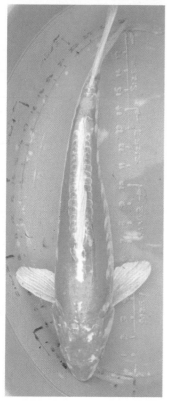

Kikusui: A beautiful fish of a platinum colour, which is particularly striking on the head and back. It has Doitsu scales along the rear of the dorsal region and irregular pale yellow markings on the body and in the fins.

Hikari-Utsurimono: Hybrids between Utsuri and Ogon families. Several two-colour varieties are available, including:

Ginshiro: A highly lustrous black on silvery platinum fish. This form is also known as Kinshiro Utsuri.

Kin Ki Utsuri: These metallic types of Ki Utsuri are very handsome Koi in black and yellow or black and orange. The former are hybrids of Ki Utsuri with Ogon and the latter are derived from crossings between Hi Utsuri and Ogon.

Below: **Ginshiro**
A fine blend of black and silver.

Below: **Kin Ki Utsuri**
An elegant Koi with a metallic glow.

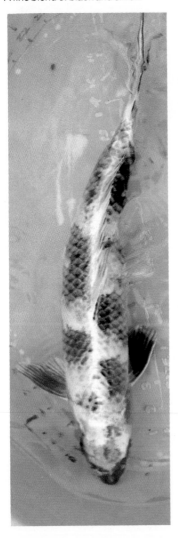

Kinginrin: Koi with numerous mother of pearl scales in either silver or gold, are designated as 'Kinginrin'. This can apply to all classes of Koi. In Kinginrin Kohaku, for example, the silver scales seen on the white portion of the Kohaku are called Ginrin, while those on the red portions are known as Kinrin. These iridescent scales can be given specific terms according to their size, texture and location.

Below: **Kinginrin Kohaku**
A Kohaku with glinting scales.

Koi colours and patterns

Aka	Red
Beni	Orange-red
Cha	Brown
Gin	Silver metallic
Hi	Red
Ki	Yellow
Kin	Gold metallic
Matsuba	Pine cone pattern
Nezu	Grey
Shiro	White
Sumi	Black

Three-colour Koi

Above: *A group photograph featuring several three-colour forms* of Koi. As the following pages show, these colour forms are principally in

the Sanke (or Sanshoku) group. The colours involved are red, black and white, although blue plays a part in the coloration of Koromo hybrids.

Three-colour Koi are known as Sanshoku or, more generally, Sanke. The two main 'classes' featured here are Taisho Sanke and Showa Sanke. The colours involved are red, black and white, although in some types blue is involved.

Taisho Sanke: This koi has Hi (red) and Sumi (black) markings on a white background. Along with the Kohaku, these fish are held in the highest esteem at Japanese shows. Judging points would be the possession of a interesting Hi mark on the head while the Hi and Sumi of the main body pattern should be distinct and well balanced. As in the Kohaku, the white should be like snow. The overall appearance should be clear and bright. Cloudy skins and/or black specks on the white are not desirable. If the fish has black on the fins or gills, the body pattern has 'stabilized'.

Tancho Sanke: The red is restricted to a large round Hi pattern – representing the rising sun – on the head. There is no red on the body, which is white with Sumi markings.

Right: **Tancho Sanke**
A fine example of a popular type.

Below: **Taisho Sanke**
A universally favoured type of Koi.

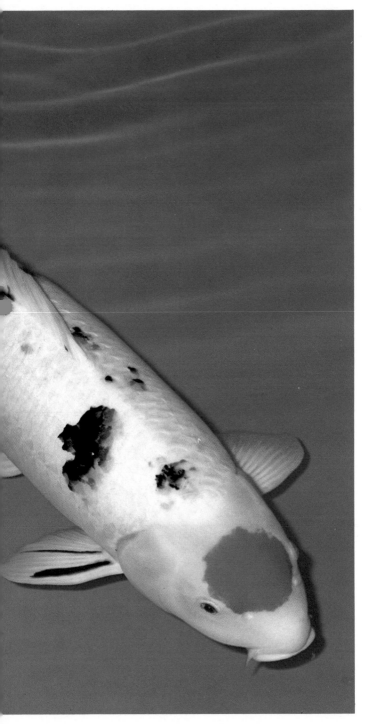

Aka Sanke: In this type the red extends from head to tail, and is overlaid with black markings.

Showa Sanke: Showa Sanke has a ground colour of black overlaid with red and white markings. As in other Koi, the colours must be clear with a distinct borderline. About twenty percent of white is desirable and this should be snow white. White markings must be present on the head, the joint of the tail and on the back. There should be a good-sized Hi mark on the head. The Sumi must be intense, forming a centrally placed lightning pattern on the back and extending over the sides of the fish and onto the abdomen.

Boke Showa: Here the Showa's back is in a netlike pattern.

Hi Showa: This fish has very little white and the Hi markings predominate on the back.

Kindai Showa: In this type the white predominates and the Sumi is relatively scarce compared with other Showas. This variety is very popular in Europe as well as Japan.

Above: **Kinginrin Showa**
A celebrated example of this Showa overlaid with a metallic sheen.

Left: **Kindai Showa**
In this form, the white is much more prominent and the black is sparse.

Right: **Hi Showa**
A striking form in which red is the dominant colour on the back.

Tancho Showa: Tancho Showa has no Hi on the body but has a Hi spot on the head.

Koromo: These hybrids of Asagi and Kohaku or Asagi and Sanke include the following four types:

Ai-Goromo: This is a cross between Asagi and Kohaku. Its Hi scales have distinctive blue borders.

Koromo-Sanke: This cross between Ai-Goromo and Taisho Sanke has blue shadows overlaying the Hi scales of a Taisho Sanke.

Budo Sanke: With blue/purple markings on the Hi.

Koromo-Showa: A cross between Ai-Goromo and Showa Sanke, with blue patches on the Hi patterns of the Showa Sanke.

Kin Showa/Gin Showa: Golden lustre specimens are Kin Showa; with a platinum lustre, Gin Showa.

Left: **Tancho Showa**
Black can appear on the head area.

Above: **Koromo (Ai-Goromo)**
These hybrids of Asagi and Kohaku are distinguished by blue patterning on the red (Hi) areas of the body.

Above: **Ai-Goromo**
The blue borders of the red (Hi)   scales produce a characteristic
netlike body pattern in this form.

Above: **Kin Showa**
A Showa type of Koi with an
appealing gold metallic lustre
derived from the influence of Ogon.

Multicoloured Koi

With the numerous crosses between Koi groupings, there are many four-coloured fish and one, the famous Goshiki, has five colours: red, white, black, blue and dark blue.

Koi groupings
The Japanese have divided Koi into the following thirteen groups based on genealogy:

Below: **Goshiki** *Five-coloured Koi.*

1 Kohaku: Shiromuji, Akamuji (Higoi, Benigoi, Hiaka), Aka Hajiro, Kuchibeni Kohaku, Nidan Kohaku, Sandan Kohaku, Yodan Kohaku, Inazuma, Straight Hi, Doitsu Kohaku, Goten-zakura, Kinzakura

2 Taisho Sanke: Kuchibeni Sanke, Aka Sanke, Doitsu Sanke, Doitsu Aka Sanke

3 Showa Sanke: Boke Showa, Hi Showa, Kindai Showa, Doitsu Showa

4 Utsurimono: Shiro Utsuri, Ki Utsuri, Hi Utsuri, Utsuri Doitsu

5 Bekko: Shiro Bekko, Aka Bekko, Ki Bekko, Bekko Doitsu

6 Asagi/Shusui: Konjo Asagi, Narumi Asagi, Mizu Asagi, Asagi Sanke, Taki Asagi, Hana Shusui, Hi Shusui

7 Koromo: Ai-goromo, Sumi-goromo, Budo Sanke, Koromo Sanke, Koromo Showa

8 Kawarimono: Karasugoi, Hajiro, Suminagashi, Matsukawabake, Kumonryu, Kigoi, Chagoi, Midorigoi, Matsuba (Aka Matsuba, Shiro Matsuba), Goshiki, Sanke Shusui, Showa Shusui, Goshiki Shusui, Kanoko Kohaku, Kanoko Sanke, Kanoko Showa, Kage Utsuri (Kage Shiro Utsuri, Kage Hi Utsuri), Kage Showa

9 Ogon: Ogon, Nezu Ogon, Parrachina/Platinum Ogon, Yamabuki Ogon, Orenji Ogon, Hi Ogon, Kin Matsuba, Gin Matsuba, Doitsu Ogon, Parrachina Doitsu, Orenji Doitsu, Mizuho Ogon, Kin Kabuto, Gin Kabuto, Kinbo, Ginbo

10 Hikarimoyo-mono: Hariwake, Yamabuki Hariwake, Orenji Hariwake, Hariwake Matsuba, Hariwake Doitsu, Kikusui, Parrachina Kohaku, Yamatonishiki, Kinsui Ginsui, Kujaku Ogon, Kujaku Doitsu, Tora Ogon

11 Hikari-Utsurimono: Kin Showa, Gin Showa, Ginshiro (Kinshiro-Utsuri), Kin Ki Utsuri

12 Kinginrin: All kinds

13 Tancho: Tancho Kohaku, Tancho Sanke, Tancho Showa

Other pond fish

The majority of fishes kept in ponds are, for obvious reasons, highly coloured, and originate from carefully cultivated domestic strains – after all, this is not only how pondkeeping as a hobby came about, but also has been a constant impetus ever since.

Although this arrangement has served pondkeepers well (and will continue to do so), bear in mind that all the decorative fishes we enjoy keeping in our ponds originally came from wild stock. However, close scrutiny of taxonomic classifications reveals that despite the many and various colour strains of Goldfish (and equally numerous different patterns of Koi), only two actual genera are involved – *Carassius auratus* and *Cyprinus carpio*. So you will not be departing from the norm to consider keeping some more of the 'wild' genera. One or two are already familiar – Golden Orfe and Golden Tench –

but increasingly others are being introduced into garden ponds.

Try to provide conditions similar to those found in the fishes' natural habitat, but remember that some fishes will prey upon others. Owners of very large ponds or lakes might well be tempted to go 'native', but many fishes kept in these circumstances become shy and elusive, and it's only when a major clean-out occurs that the fish population is re-discovered. Restricting fish to the smaller, easily observed pond, seems to be the answer; certainly 'tiddlers' are much better off in small ponds – provided you can keep the conditions to their liking. There are laws governing the taking of fish from the wild, and there is also a moral responsibility upon the pondkeeper not to introduce cultivated fishes in the opposite direction, should they outgrow their garden pond home.

Golden Orfe
(*Idus idus*)

This fish is lively and provides a lot of interest in the pond. If kept as a single fish or in a single pair it is shy and rarely seen, but in a shoal it is much more confident, moving quickly and darting out in the open areas of water, and rising to take food from the surface. It is a small hardy fish with a pale golden colour that fades to silver as it nears the dorsal curve, the fins retaining a stronger colour; a silver variety is also available.

The Golden Orfe is long and slender, reaching 30cm (12in) in length. It is an excellent scavenger, removing insects and mosquito larvae from plants and from the water surface. It is best kept in a spacious pond where it can have a good length to swim in; it has been known to jump right out of small ponds. During the winter months it is less active and keeps away from the surface, preferring to lie dormant near the pond bottom.

Above: *Golden Orfe, a very popular fish that is fast and spectacular when kept in a shoal, but shy when kept as a pair or a single fish.*

Golden Rudd
(*Scardinius erythrophthalmus*)
This very attractive fish has a silvery colour with a golden hue. The scales are large, rough and distinct. The eyes and fins are red, and the pectoral, pelvic and anal fins are darker than the dorsal fin. It is often confused with the Roach (*Rutilus rutilus*), but is distinguishable because its dorsal fin starts well back on the spine, between the anal and pelvic fins.

The Golden Rudd will grow to 45cm (18in) in length, and may reach 2kg (4lb 6oz) in weight. It feeds on worms and ant eggs as well as aquatic vegetation. It is found wild in slow-running rivers and lakes in most parts of Europe. The Golden Rudd lays eggs among weeds, and they

Left: *Golden Rudd can grow to quite a large size for a garden pond; 45cm (18in) long and 2kg (4lb 6oz) in weight. It is hardy and attractive.*

hatch in five to eight days. It is quite like the Golden Orfe, of a better shape but not so bright in colour. This hardy species thrives in the open pond , where it lives well with other fishes.

Golden Tench
(*Tinca tinca*)
This very hardy fish will live a long time out of water. It grows well and increases quickly in still water, which it prefers to running water. The skin is slimy and this is reputed to cure various diseases on other fishes in the pond. Its natural food consists of insects, worms and young shoots of water vegetation. It will increase quickly where the conditions are right, and two males should be provided for each female; the sexes can be distinguished by the size of the pelvic fin, which is larger in the male. The mouth has a barbel on each side.

This fish is dark green in colour, with pink lips and very dark green fins. When mature it may reach a length of 45cm (18in), and weigh up to 2.5kg (5lb 8oz). These fishes are excellent scavengers as they always eat off the bottom of the pond. They are often found in rivers, ponds and sand pits.

Minnow
(Phoxinus phoxinus)
These small fishes are found in the wild in many streams, ponds and rivers, and they readily settle into pond life. They prefer to live in shoals, where they are very active and give plenty of movement to the water. They live for quite a long time, and individuals have been known to survive for 12 years in a pond. In spring the male minnow changes colour from its original olive-brown to a green flushed with red. The female will spawn on gravel, and the eggs hatch in about ten days.

With a change in the surroundings Minnows will change colour, turning lighter or darker according to the background. The dorsal fin is placed well back, over the space between the pectoral and anal fins. The tail is forked, with large spots at the base. The fish has a total length of some 7.5cm (3in). Minnows are hardy, and bold in taking food from larger fishes; they enjoy flies, meat and worms.

Grass Carp
(Ctenopharyngodon idella)
Grass Carp may seem the ideal fish to help keep down any growths of algae in the pond, but they do not restrict their appetite to this alone and will also eat oxygenating plants with relish. As they can grow to well over 90cm (36in), and may leap out of the pond as well, they may not be a prudent choice for a pond after all.

Sunfishes and Basses
These North American fishes vary greatly in size, from the Pigmy Everglades Sunfish (*Elassoma evergladei*) to the very large Black Bass (*Micropterus dolomieu*); other genera include *Centrarchus, Enneacanthus, Lepomis* and *Pomoxis*. Admirable features of

Below: A shoal of tiny minnows provides a flash of movement in the pond. Their colours change according to their surroundings.

most species are the iridescent dots on the flanks and interesting breeding patterns; less welcome are the predatory tendencies developed by most larger species.

Above: *Male pigmy Everglades Sunfish turn jet black when breeding.*

Below: *the Pumpkinseed Sunfish's shining scales are unseen in the pond.*

Shiners and Darters

The colourful genera *Notropis* and *Etheostoma* from North America are perhaps more suitable for ponds in summer. The Red Shiner *(Notropis lutrensis)* is an active, brightly coloured violet-hued fish with red fins. During the breeding season, red areas on the head and behind the gills intensify, and males develop small white tubercles on the head. The Red Shiner needs clean, well-oxygenated water with an upper temperature of around 22°C (70°F). Being an active fish, it may not always be an ideal companion for slower-moving Goldfish, often nipping at their fins.

Darters (*Etheostoma spp*) are small brightly coloured fishes inhabiting well-oxygenated running waters. Similar in appearance to gobies, they require a rocky substrate in which they can hide. They are suitable for the smaller pond, and some enterprising pondkeepers have tried keeping them in watercourses between ponds, to simulate their natural conditions more exactly. But such shallow conditions will tend to make them easy prey for cats.

Mudminnows

Although some native species may be too dull in colour for inclusion in the pond (and mudminnows of the genus *Umbra* are no exception), the Rosy, or Fat-Headed Minnow (*Pimephales promelas*) is a pinky yellow fish, which will show up more clearly. Despite coming from temperate climates, some mudminnows still need to be brought in for the winter.

Catfish

Catfish have gained an unfair reputation for being obliging scavengers, constantly patrolling the bottom clearing up everybody else's leftovers. Although this may be true to a certain extent, the introduction of catfish into a garden pond is not recommended.

Left: *The Red Shiner* (Notropis lutrensis) *is a lively, colourful addition to the summertime pond.*

Right: *Although aggressive, the Three-spined Stickleback is worth keeping for its breeding behaviour.*

Below: *The tropical White Cloud Mountain Minnow can be kept outdoors during summer months.*

Most grow too big, with a predatory appetite to match; apart from the obvious risk to smaller pondfish, the real problem comes when the pondkeeper has to find a responsible method of disposing of them. The nearest ornamental park lake is *not* the answer, nor is the local river or canal.

Sticklebacks

The Three-spined Stickleback (*Gasterosteus aculeatus*) is another fish familiar to all children, and it has an unusual breeding method. The male constructs a nest or tunnel of plant material into which he coaxes the female; eggs are laid by the female and fertilized by the male, which then stands guard over the nest, fanning water currents over the eggs until they hatch. Males, in their bright red breeding garb, are quite aggressive at spawning times.

The Ten-spined Stickleback (*Pungitius pungitius*) has a similar lifestyle to the Three-spined Stickleback, but may be less aggressive. The male turns black at breeding times.

Short-stay fishes

A pond in summer can provide excellent extension living quarters for tropical fishes, which will benefit from the extra room to stretch their fins and a good supply of real live aquatic foods.

Livebearing fishes, such as mollies, will certainly benefit from any natural algae in the pond, as will swordtails, but remember that water temperatures must remain constantly reasonably high for the fish to thrive.

Some 'tropicals', however, do not always require as high a temperature as their aquarium companions, and will cope very well with slightly cooler conditions. Typical examples are the American Flagfish (*Jordanella floridae*), the Japanese Rice-fish (*Oryzias latipes*) and White Cloud Mountain Minnows (*Tanichthys albonubes*).

Appendix 1: Other pond livestock

Apart from the livestock deliberately introduced into the water, other forms creep in uninvited, but most of these are beneficial, either keeping the pond clean or providing a ready meal for the fishes. Others are more trouble, however, causing damage to fish and plant life, especially the small fry and the young fresh growth; it is important to keep an eye on the health of the pond life and spot any damage to fishes or plants that may have been caused by an unwanted guest. Among the vast amount of livestock it is quite difficult to determine which is friend and which is foe, and it is impossible to keep an outdoor pond free from the visitations of insects and other life forms.

Snails

One of the few animals that needs to be introduced into the pond is the snail. There are a number of aquatic snails that will happily feed on debris and help to keep the pond clean without feeding on the plant life.

Planorbis corneus (the Ramshorn Snail) can be put into the pool to clean up unwanted rubbish. It is easily recognized by its handsome flat coiled shell, and breeds well. It will not damage useful vegetation, and is readily available from aquatic dealers.

Viviparus viviparus (the Freshwater Winkle) delights in feeding on dead and decaying vegetation, and is popular with fishkeepers. If disturbed it will cling very tightly to whatever it is attached to, resisting any attempt to pull it off, no matter how hard.

Viviparus fasciatus is very similar to *V. viviparus*, and also eats decaying plant life; but it is also completely different, in that it releases itself the moment it is touched.

Most of the other snails that are found in the pond introduce themselves and can be left to populate the water unless they are seen to feed on your prize aquatics. Some are small and insignificant, others are larger. Some of the bigger snails are from the

Below: *The Common Frog,* Rana temporaria, *is a welcome visitor to the pool, often consuming unwanted pests such as slugs and snails.*

Lymnaea family, which includes the Great Pond Snail (*Lymnaea stagnalis*), a snail that through indiscriminate feeding can cause a lot of damage and should be removed.

Amphibians

Amphibians visit the pond to lay their eggs or spawn; some fishkeepers find

Below: *The Common Toad,* Bufo bufo, *will lay spawn in the spring, but any disadvantage is outweighed by the insects that they consume.*

Above: *Common or Smooth Newt,* Triturus vulgaris, *comes to the pond to breed in spring and summer.*

the spawn unsightly and remove it, but the young are beneficial to the balance of life in the water. Young tadpoles are excellent scavengers, starting off by eating vegetable matter and progressing to animal foods. Frogs, toads and newts should all be welcome because they do so much good in the garden, removing unwanted pests such as insects.

Above: *A Dragonfly performs very swift and agile movements in flight which, coupled with its brilliant colouring, gives any pool interest.*

Below: *There are many varieties of Caddis Fly, most of which have interesting larvae that form homes of fine particles of stone or shell.*

Beetles and other insects

There are well over 200 different species of aquatic beetle; some of these are savage and carnivorous, attacking fish and other water animals, but most are happy scavenging among the debris and keeping the pond clean. Unless attacks are seen, it is best to leave most beetles alone.

Surface walkers are often seen traversing the water relying on the surface tension to stop themselves sinking. The best-known of these is *Gerris najas* (the Pond Skater), which literally walks across the water on the lookout for dead or dying insects.

There are a large number of flies that leave their eggs in or close to water, from the humble midges and gnats to the larger caddis flies and dragonflies. Their eggs turn into larvae that prey on lower water creatures, other larvae and tiny fishes, and they in turn become food for larger fishes. There are over 160 different kinds of caddis fly. One of the commonest is *Phryganea grandis* with pale grey-brown wings and yellow-ringed antennae; it folds its wings along its body when at rest, like all the caddis flies. Their larvae form cases or tubes from fine particles of vegetation, stones, sand or shell to live in until the next stage in their development into flying insects.

The dragonflies form a large group of insects well-known for their spectacular colouring and erratic flight pattern. Their eggs are laid on the water surface and then sink to the bottom. When the larvae are hatched they form burrows in which they lie low, preying on small aquatic animal life; then they gradually change until they eventually become flying insects. Dragonfly larvae (nymphs) can be considered a pest and are further described on page 104. Among the other flies are *Culex pipiens* (the Common Gnat) and *Chaoborus* sp. (the Midge). The larvae of these are a good food for fishes, and anyone who fails to keep fishes in the garden pond is likely to become aware of a subsequent noticeable increase in the gnat and midge population.

Other freshwater creatures
Among the other forms of water life is *Argyroneta aquatica* (the Water Spider), which manages to live and nest under water without drowning, due to the air secreted between the hairs on its body; it feeds on land and aquatic animals. Aquatic worms such as *Tubifex* are very similar to the common earthworm, but of a transparent red colour; they provide a useful source of food for the rest of the pond's carnivorous animals. Among the crustaceans that live in fresh water is *Gammarus* sp. (the Freshwater Shrimp), which is a good scavenger and provides food for fishes, particularly trout. *Asellus* sp. (the Water Louse) is another scavenger, and lives on decaying vegetable matter.

Above: *The Red-eyed Damselfly is a lesser form of Dragonfly that provides interest around the pool with its colouring and erratic flight pattern. It lays eggs in the water, many of which then become food for fish.*

Pests

The largest pest is usually the heron, a fishing bird with a decidedly fine taste for garden pond fishes; it arrives just after dawn and clears a pond of prize fishes before the owner is awake. Some keepers cover their pond with a fine net, placed well above the surface to prevent the bird's beak from going through the mesh and spearing the fishes. Whether it is the difficulty of reaching a fish and swallowing it through the net, or the fear that the bird is going to be caught in the mesh, is not really known, but most pond owners find this method effective. Another and less unsightly remedy is to restrict the bird's flight path; poles placed close together will prevent the wings from spreading, and encourage the bird to look for an easier and safer meal. Black thread stretched over the pond and its surround can achieve a similar effect without spoiling the look of the pond.

Cats too are attracted to the movement and flavour of garden fishes. They can be prevented by netting, or by a pet dog. A quick shower of cold water from a garden hose is a harmless deterrent.

Insect pests
Most of the insect life found in ponds is in some way harmful to plants or fishes, but this is part of nature and provided the damage is minimal the whole cycle of life will continue. But where there is some imbalance, and one insect becomes too numerous, then remedial action is necessary.

Several types of beetles and their larvae can be considered pests in the garden pond. One to look out for is the Great Diving Beetle, *Dytiscis marginalis*. It is hard to miss this rapacious predator; the adult may grow to a length of 4cm (1.6in), its dark brown oval body sometimes margined in yellow. Using its powerful mandibles, this beetle will rapidly and with the utmost of selfless ferocity attack fishes larger than itself. The larva, up to 5cm (2in) in length, is even more voracious.

Among the harmful water bugs that are able to fly from pond to pond are the so-called Water Boatmen or Backswimmers, *Notonecta* sp., easily recognizable by their upside-down swimming action just beneath the water's surface. *Notonecta glauca*, up to 1.5cm (0.6in) long, is the most commonly seen species. The Water Scorpion, *Nepa cinerea*, also attacks fishes and tadpoles. Up to 3cm (1.2in) long, this water bug has a terminal tube that it uses for breathing and is easily mistaken for a scorpion-like sting. All these water bugs and beetles are difficult to eliminate.

In many cases, it is the larval stages that pose the strongest threat to pond fishes. This is certainly true of Dragonflies, for their larvae (nymphs) lie low in submerged burrows and pounce on pond creatures that venture too close. They will attack fishes up to their own length – about 5cm (2in) – and are difficult to eradicate.

Leeches
Among those parasites that can be accidentally introduced with fishes or plants are the leeches. These worm-like animals are common in fresh water and grip their victims by means of suckers at each end of the body. They suck blood and may leave wounds that weaken the fishes and make them susceptible to other infections. Several treatments for these parasites are now commonly available. Many of them, however, are specific to single forms of pond life.

Fish lice, anchor worm and flukes
Fish lice (*Argulus* sp.) and anchor worms (*Lernaea cyprinacea*) are both parasitic crustaceans that grip onto or burrow into the fish's skin. The disc-shaped fish louse reaches up to 8mm (0.3in) in diameter and has two large gripping suckers. The anchor worm, up to 2cm (0.8in) long, penetrates the body tissue by means of jagged anchor-like appendages and can cause considerable wounds.

Both these parasites may cause affected fish to swim rapidly around the pond. Similar 'distress symptoms' are also seen in fishes carrying gill flukes (*Dactylogyrus* sp). These are flatworm parasites up to 0.8mm (0.03in) long that attach themselves to the gill membranes. Skin flukes (*Gyrodactylus*) may also cause problems. Use an anti-parasite remedy for both these flukes.

Black spot

This is caused by the sucking worm *Neodiplostomum cuticola*. In this case it is the larval stage that produces the symptoms – brown or black spots on the body or fins. Each spot is an encysted larva. This parasite may be introduced by snails or visiting birds, and is best treated with an anti-parasite remedy.

Below: *The main pests to look for. Top left: Aphids on aquatic plants can carry diseases. Right: Water beetles can damage plants and attack fish.*

Plant pests

Aquatic plants, particularly water lilies, can become infested with aphids and other small insects. If your pond is well stocked with fishes, just push the leaves under the water and rest a piece of wood over them to keep the leaves immersed. The fishes will eat the pests, and the leaves can then be released.

Bottom row, left to right: *The Anchor Worm, Dragonfly larvae and Fish Louse will all attack or attach themselves to fish, causing damage.*

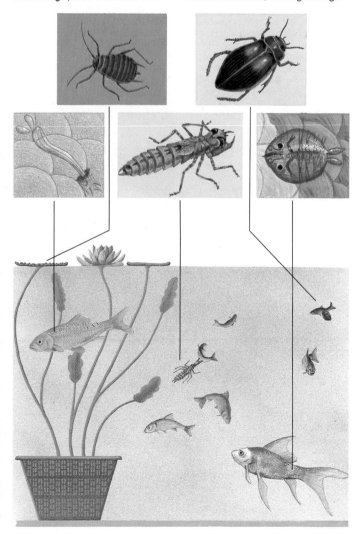

Appendix 2: A seasonal diary

Spring

Spring shows itself when the bulbs begin to appear and the fishes in the pond begin to stir, rising to the surface and moving in search of food. You can start to feed them but give only a very little at a time; use the floating pellets so that you can be sure that no more are given than the fishes can eat in five minutes or so. The first flowers of the aquatics should be blooming, usually *Caltha palustris* (the Marsh Marigold) in both single and double forms. The water lilies should be making growth, sending up shoots through the water. Frogs and other amphibians will begin to mate and spread their spawn in the shallow parts of the pond.

As the fishes have used up most of their reserves of nutrition they have little resistance to disease, particularly fungus infections. They need to be nurtured until their energy increases, and then their food should be supplemented with minced earthworms and scraps of meat and vegetables. Give the fishes as much as they will eat to bring them up to good condition ready for breeding.

Sometimes the decaying vegetation and the plant growth of the oxygenators and other aquatics that died back during the winter make the water coloured, sometimes black and at other times cloudy. This is more likely to happen in small ponds where there has been a prolific aquatic plant growth. The decaying matter should be removed where possible, and a partial water change is often necessary. There are two basic methods of changing the water. The easiest is to allow the fresh water to trickle in from a hosepipe and the excess water to overflow the edge of the pond very gently; this is fine where the surrounding soil is quick-draining and the water will not cause any hazard. The alternative is to drain half the water out of the pond into a soakaway or drain by using a pump and hose. Once the pond is down to half full the hose can be attached to the tap and adjusted to give a gentle trickle. If your tap water is highly chlorinated, get a dechlorinator from your aquarist suppliers, to make the water more palatable for the fishes.

The trickle action will give the water time to adjust to the surrounding temperature.

While the pool is at a low ebb, it is wise to take out and check the plant life. Baskets can be raised, and where the plants are too rampant divide and replant them. Replace weak plants, and remove those that are too vigorous and tall, putting smaller-growing varieties in their place.

Equipment removed in the autumn can be checked and put back into the pond. Examine everything for wear, and the cables for chafing or cracking, replacing where necessary. Check the connections to make sure

that they are secure. Grease the pins on plugs to ensure a good contact, and service pumps and lights if they require it. Check light bulbs and replace any that do not work. Clean out the filter, and see that the impeller on the pump is working freely; then start the pump working for a short while to make sure that everything is in order for the summer. After the danger of frost has passed, the pool heater can be removed and stored for the summer. Clean netting of old leaves, and restretch it to keep off herons and cats; make sure that the edges are well secured as these predators have been known to lift a loose end and enjoy a free meal of fish in comparative freedom.

When feeding plants around the perimeter of the pond, take care to prevent any spillage of fertilizer into the water, as it will encourage algae. It is better to use a natural organic food such as well-rotted manure or a liquid feed based on seaweed rather than a chemically based one that may leave excess nitrates in the soil that can seep into the pond water.

Below: *Spring flowers and emerging growth show the beginnings of a fresh season: the time to check the plants and start feeding the fish.*

Summer

Summer is the time to enjoy the pond, to watch the action and movement, to savour the fragrance of the flowers and listen to the sounds of water and insect life. The various aquatics are flowering; the water lilies start in warm weather with their cup-shaped flowers on and above the water surface, the marginals and bog plants a little less spectacularly.

Some plants need thinning during the summer months to prevent them from becoming too large for their allotted space. When this entails lifting the basket to cut back side shoots or to divide it, the water becomes muddy, and this can take a day or two to settle. But switch on the pump for the fountain or waterfall, and the filter will strain out the silt, so that the water will become less cloudy within an hour or two. New plants can be settled in, and old ones tidied up and fed with aquatic fertilizer pellets to boost their growth, especially the water lilies. Where insects have attacked leaves just above the water surface, push down the affected parts under the water and rest a plank or weight on them to keep them immersed while the fishes eat the insects as a bonus live feed.

This is the time of year when a rapid and unexpected growth of filamentous algae – usually called blanket weed – can occur, even in ponds that have been free from it for

Above: *The splash of moving water with the colour and scent of flowers on a hot summer's day is only part of the reward for having a pool.*

Left: *Lush green growth of waterside plants will attract colourful insects on hot days, and cool the oppressive heat of the midsummer sun.*

decades. Some say that this is due to amphibians arriving at the pond with tiny strands of the weed caught round their legs or bodies from another pond; when they swim the strand becomes loose and spreads speedily in its new environment. Insert a stout pole into the mass of green leaf and turn it; like a fork in a plateful of spaghetti, it will gather up all the weed, which can then be lifted out and removed.

The fishes become more active and need a supplement to their food if the insect life is not too prolific; but do not allow the food to stay in the pond to spoil and pollute the water. If the fishes have spawned and the tiny fry are seen swimming about, separate the young from their parents to prevent their being eaten. Take out the fry with a very fine net and keep them in a separate pond until they are large enough to rejoin their parents. New fishes should be kept in quarantine before being released into the pond; the plastic bag in which they have travelled should be immersed in a container or a separate pond until it is certain that the fishes are healthy and vigorous, when they can be moved into the main pond. One diseased fish can cause havoc in an otherwise healthy pond.

If evaporation occurs during hot weather the level should be topped up and the fountain or waterfall should be working most of the time.

Autumn

Plants are beginning to look tired, and as soon as the first frost occurs many will be cut back. This is the time to remove dead withering leaves and growth, and seed heads should be removed unless you want the plants to seed. The plants in the pond, particularly those with leaves under the surface, should be cut well back

Below: *At the end of the winter the pool hints at the promise of spring with fresh growth just emerging.*

Above: *In winter the spectacle of frost and ice is beautiful, but some water should be kept open for fish.*

and the growth removed. The exceptions to this are the evergreen plants, which should have their dying leaves removed. This will lessen any decay of plant life in the pond and avoid upsetting its balance. Spent leaves and blooms of water lilies should also be removed. Any tender plants that will not survive the frost must be lifted and removed to a frost-

free place. The pond should be cleared of rotting vegetation.

Fishes should be fattened up; give them plenty of food so that they can have a good store of nutrients to help them through the winter months. They should still be active as long as the weather remains warm, but make sure that no food is left in the water to decompose.

Check that the edges of the pond net are secure, and that it will catch any leaves that fall towards the pond and also deter predators from trying

to catch the fish. As cooler weather comes, the fishes will be less active. The more delicate specimens should be carefully lifted out and put into a frost-free pond or aquarium indoors for the winter. As most of the natural cover for the fishes has now been removed or allowed to die back, some form of shelter is essential to give them protection during the winter months when they are slow and in a near hibernation state – an ideal quarry for a predator. Lay a series of inert drain pipes on the pool bottom, in which the fishes will be able to hide and remain secure from the attentions of herons and cats. Protect pond-side plants that are not quite hardy by covering them with a layer of bracken or straw.

Winter
In cold weather the fishes need less oxygen and food, and they rest in a state of torpor gradually using up the food stored as layers of fat. When the pond freezes over it keeps oxygen from reaching the water and prevents the toxic gases from leaving it. For the most part the cold is only sufficient for the pond to be frozen over for a few hours, and this is not a hazard to the pond inhabitants. Only when it is covered with ice for a number of days does trouble start to build up.

A pond heater is an ideal answer; drop it into the water, where its float will bring it to the surface. The little power that it uses – the equivalent of an electric-light bulb – will be sufficient to keep an area of water free from ice. Switch it on only when frost is forecast, and keep it on in times of prolonged freezing. An alternative is to fill a can with boiling water and rest it on the ice, which will soon melt. Remove some of the water from under the ice, to leave a gap for air to get in and for the gases to get out.

Remove and clean pumps, then store them for the winter should the makers advise it. If a pump is left in the pond it is important to run it for a few minutes every week or so, to keep the machine parts free and working well. Pond lights should also be removed and cleaned; remove algae from the glass, check the wiring, and store the lights for the whole winter period.

Appendix 3: Pond problem solving

How can I effectively rid the pond of green water, algae and blanketweed?

The many established methods of dealing with algae-associated problems have varying success rates. **Algicides** need to be used with care – the vital thing is getting the dosage correct – a very difficult thing to do unless you know the exact volume of your pond. The resulting amount of dead algae will lead to extreme oxygen starvation in the pond unless it is removed. The new liquid remedies are very effective against algae problems as long as manufacturers' instructions are followed precisely. **Blanketweed** need not be too tiresome, providing you remove it immediately it begins to form. Most filters cannot remove the tiny cells that produce the effect of **green water** by simply straining them out. However, the use of **ultra-violet light** coupled with a foam filter medium is more efficient, as the UV amalgamates the cells together into large 'blobs', so that normal filter medium can trap them easily.

The best defence against green water is to prevent it forming in the first place: provide fast-growing plants to compete for the nutrients, and partially shade the surface with water lilies. Immersible bags of special soils or peat extracts have also proved effective.

If fish seem to be hanging at the surface, is there anything wrong?

Generally, the appearance of fish congregating at the water surface, except at feeding times, is either a sign that there is an oxygen deficiency in the water, or else that the fish cannot make use of any oxygen that is there; by coming to the surface they can take in some atmospheric air. Oxygen deficiency is likely during periods of very warm weather: fountains should be left running to further aerate the water. If the fish are at the surface in the early morning there may be too many plants in the pond, which, although producing oxygen during the day, actually compete for it, against the fishes, during the night, and also produce excessive carbon dioxide.

If there is enough oxygen in the water it may be that the fish are affected by gill flukes, which coat the fish's gill membranes and prevent oxygen absorption.

Will overhanging trees pose any danger to a pond?

In short, all nearby trees can pose a danger to ponds. Starting at the bottom, their roots can penetrate liners and crack concrete; their leaves and fruit will fall into the pond and pollute the water (worse still they could be poisonous); they could blow over into the pond during a storm, and they will prevent sunshine reaching the pond, so that plants, especially water lilies, will not thrive.

Will frogs and toads harm the fish?

The only real danger to fish is when over-amorous frogs and toads clasp them during the breeding season, but a fast-swimming fish can generally escape such attentions. Fish will eat frog tadpoles but ignore those of the toad. The presence of seasonal amphibious life in and around the pond is to be encouraged, as many garden pests, such as slugs and insects, will be kept under control by newts, frogs and toads.

Right: The water-sterilizing ultra-violet lamp (housed in the dark tune to prevent eye damage) is easily replaced when necessary.

Above: *Despite their collective visual appeal, trees and ponds are not always good companions unless you can prevent water pollution.*

When is the best time to clean out the pond?

Either spring or autumn is a good time but, on balance, autumn has the advantage in that any decaying plant matter is removed before winter, during which time it would otherwise have produced toxic gases. It is a good idea to minimize the accumulation of fallen leaves in the pond by covering the pond with a small-mesh net during autumn. Divide water lily rhizomes at this time, if they have become too large or outgrown their containers. During the cleaning out operation the fish should be kept in containers filled with pond water; don't forget that you will need to treat the new pond water with dechlorinators when refilling.

How can I trace a leak from the pond?

First of all, make sure the water loss is occurring directly from the pond, and not from misaligned or clogged cascades, split waterfall supply hoses, or mis-sited or tilted fountains. Then, once the water remains at a steady unchanging level, check around the water-line for a hole in the liner or fibreglass, or crack in the concrete. Liner and fibreglass ponds can be repaired fairly simply with the appropriate repair kit, but patching concrete is more difficult – in this case, it may be better to re-line the whole pond.

How often should I feed my fish?

It's not so much how often, but how much, that is important. Fish such as Goldfish and Koi feed constantly (they have no stomach as such in which to store or digest food), and from late spring to autumn they can be fed 'little and often' once the water temperature remains constantly above 10°C (50°F). Make sure that all the food given is eaten within a few minutes; one advantage of floating pellet foods is that you can see just how much the fish have, or haven't eaten, and adjust the amount accordingly. Koi need a diet change to higher-content vegetable foods (wheatgerm) during autumn.

My fish are chasing each other, what should I do?

Give yourself a congratulatory pat on the back – the fish are obviously content in your pond, because they are spawning! The males will drive the females vigorously in among the plants, especially in the shallow water where it is warmer. You may be able to see eggs sticking to the plants after all the chasing is over.

Remove the plants to a separate hatching pond (or aquarium) if you want to save a large proportion of fry, as many of the eggs (and newly hatched fry) will be eaten if left in the pond.

Does the pond have to be fully protected against ice?
The most important thing during winter is to keep the pond ventilated, by preventing ice from completely sealing in any toxic gases. The formation of such gases can be minimized by clearing out decaying plant matter from the pond during autumn. An open area in the ice should be maintained by using a floating pond heater, or an anchored polystyrene ventilated bell, which keeps a volume of warm air over one area of the pond, and prevents ice from forming.

Leaving a pump running may actually lower the overall water temperature by preventing the natural stratification that otherwise sets up a safe warmer (4°C/39°F) layer at the bottom of the pond.

How can I keep herons and cats out of the pond?
Small low fences, netting and trip-threads may do the trick, as will any other natural obstacles (plants, shrubs etc) that prevent easy access to the pond. Plastic life-size replicas of herons may prove effective, and small electrified wire systems, or loud electronically generated noises triggered off by tripwires have all been tried. Floating plastic water-lily leaves (which quickly sink under the weight of any predatory cat's paw) provide a more natural-looking deterrent.

What's the difference between submersible and surface pumps?
Submersible pumps operate in the pond, while surface pumps are sited on dry land. Submersible pumps are mostly used with fountain kits (the jets sit on top of the pump), but many models also have a 'T' piece attachment to feed an external filter as well.

Surface pumps can deliver large volumes of water (ideal for waterfalls), but need to be installed in a weather-proof housing (as do transformers for any low-voltage pump system) and require regular inspection and maintenance.

What are the different types of pond filter?
The pond can have internal and external filtration systems just like an aquarium. **Internal** types, such as biological filters, are best installed during construction, as are gravity-fed external systems, which are usually sited immediately alongside the pond. More basic internal filters are merely banks of foam cartridges

Above: *When is a heron not a heron? When it's a plastic replica set up to deter the real thing. Actual effectiveness is difficult to assess.*

fitted around a fountain pump; a sure sign that this type of filter needs cleaning is when your fountain starts to droop!

The design of most 'add-on' **external filters** centres around small plastic household water cisterns – fittings are inexpensive and easily obtainable. Water is pumped into the filter, passes either upwards or downwards through a foam sheet, and returns by gravity to the pond. It is fairly simple to build multi-chamber versions with each chamber having a different medium: filter brushes, or a biological chamber filled with anything from proprietary materials to plastic hair-curlers! Back flushing and drainage taps are easily fitted; the most recent models incorporate a UV lamp to further clarify the water. A common place to hide such a filter is in the pondside rockery, but remember to allow easy access for regular maintenance.

What size biological filter will I need for my pond?
The bigger the better, but a biological filter bed housed within a pond should cover at least a third of the pond's base area. The gravel bed can be contained within a walled-off area to prevent it being spread too thinly over the pond base by foraging fishes.

What are the advantages of low-voltage operated pond equipment over the mains-voltage type?
Without a doubt, the biggest advantage is safety, but there is an additional installation complication with low-voltage equipment, as the necessary 'step-down' transformer has to be sited somewhere – not in the pond! If the transformer has a large enough rating, other low-voltage devices (lighting etc) may be run from the same unit.

Whatever system is used, the question of electrical safety cannot be stressed too strongly. Switches and junction boxes must be suitable for outdoor use; armoured supply cables must be used, or cables sheathed in protective piping before burying. An earth-trip, or circuit-breaker is also a wise inclusion.

Is there any advantage in building a raised pond rather than a traditional sunken type?
Apart from not having to dig a hole, a raised pond has other advantages – it can be maintained more easily; it can be more practical for disabled people (or youngsters) who can approach its edges safely without fear of toppling in, and fish can be seen easily from a sitting position, from a wheelchair for example. Such ponds can look a little unnatural, but a well-designed raised patio pond looks just great. A raised pond may suffer more from frost unless well-insulated. The sunken pond is probably more natural-looking, and the usual practice is to use the excavated earth to make a rockery.

I wish to install a pond but can't decide which is the best type of construction.
Informal shapes are much easier to fabricate from liners than in concrete. Pre-fabricated shapes are often available only in small or medium sizes, but have the advantage that they can be set in the ground or raised.

Very large formal designs are better constructed in concrete and liners, although excessive ground-movement may preclude the use of concrete.

PVC liners are cheapest but any exposed portions of the liner will suffer damage from sunlight's UV rays. Butyl rubber is far superior and carries a long-term guarantee.

What's the best and easiest way to drain a pond?
Providing you are willing to expend some energy at the very outset, the answer must be via a bottom drain to a soakaway. If your pond doesn't have a drain, then a small pump attachment fitted to an electric drill will speed up the process, and a 'pond-vac', will make very short work of the task.

GENERAL INDEX

SPECIES INDEX

PICTURE CREDITS

Artists
Copyright of the artwork illustrations on the pages following the artists' names is the property of Salamander Books Ltd.

Janos Marffy: 84-85, 88-89, 90-1,

Dee McLain (Linden Artists): 18, 20-21, 22-23, 24-25, 27, 28

Clifford and Wendy Meadway: 46-47, 48, 62-63, 78-79, 86-87, 92-93, 94-95, 110-111, 112, 114, 116, 223

Colin Newman (Linden Artists): 98-99, 100-101, 102-103, 104-105, 106-107, 108-109, 118-119, 120-121, 134, 140-141

David Papworth; 65, 66-67, 68, 70-71, 74-75, 76-77

Eric Tenney: 172-173

Brian Watson (Linden Artists): 130, 131, 160, 163

Jane Winton: 51, 52, 53, 55, 72-73

Photographers
The publishers wish to thank the following photographers and agencies who have supplied photographs for this book. The photographs have been credited by page number and position on the page: (B) Bottom, (T) Top, (C) Centre, (BL) Bottom Left etc.

James Allison: 55, 58, 230

Dr. Chris Andrews: 147(T), 162

Ranunculus – *a popular pond plant.*